Confrontation

T0087487

Confrontation

Alain Badiou
Alain Finkielkraut

A Conversation with Aude Lancelin

Translated by Susan Spitzer

polity

First published in English as *L'Explication* © Nouvelles Éditions Lignes, 2010

This English edition © Polity Press, 2014

Polity Press
65 Bridge Street
Cambridge CB2 1UR, UK

Polity Press
350 Main Street
Malden, MA 02148, USA

All rights reserved. Except for the quotation of short passages for the purpose of criticism and review, no part of this publication may be reproduced, stored in a retrieval system, or transmitted, in any form or by any means, electronic, mechanical, photocopying, recording or otherwise, without the prior permission of the publisher.

ISBN-13: 978-0-7456-8569-4
ISBN-13: 978-0-7456-8570-0 (pb)

A catalogue record for this book is available from the British Library.

Typeset in 11 on 14 pt Sabon by Servis Filmsetting Ltd, Stockport, Cheshire
Printed and bound in Great Britain by T.J. International, Padstow, Cornwall

The publisher has used its best endeavours to ensure that the URLs for external websites referred to in this book are correct and active at the time of going to press. However, the publisher has no responsibility for the websites and can make no guarantee that a site will remain live or that the content is or will remain appropriate.

Every effort has been made to trace all copyright holders, but if any have been inadvertently overlooked the publisher will be pleased to include any necessary credits in any subsequent reprint or edition.

For further information on Polity, visit our website: politybooks.com

Contents

Foreword

by Aude Lancelin

"We should never debate," Philippe Muray once said. "An original thinking of the world can and must be fired off like a definitive dissent, a temperamental incompatibility. We shouldn't argue; we should cut right to the heart of the matter."[1] A brilliant essayist who wrote about the "end of History" and the all-pervasive simulacrum, Muray, the author of *Désaccord parfait* [Perfect Disagreement], had understood and articulated better than anyone else how transcending opinions is by no means the aim of most of the fake, media-driven debates today. Rather, their unwitting purpose is the evaporation of meaning. We see this sort of thing every day, moreover: the big media machine thrives on cartoonish, grossly exaggerated, if not outright made-up, conflicts, the better to divert attention from the real struggles going on. Let me just say how right my dear friend, who passed away suddenly in 2006, was once again. We should indeed never debate if it's only a pretext for creating a sham battlefield of that sort, a convenient cover

---

[1] Philippe Muray, *Moderne contre moderne: exorcismes spirituels IV* (Paris: Les Belles Lettres, 2005), 163–4.

for the inability either to act or to think. Still less should we debate if it's only a pretext for popularizing two weak viewpoints, each trying to give the other a boost to get heard – or, even worse, to attract a lot of attention.

There could be no question of any such thing happening with the two men here. Badiou and Finkielkraut represent two radically different visions that touch the very nerve of our time. Their names sound like two *noms de guerre* for two intellectual factions that are resolutely determined to fight it out with each other in France today. In fact, the first time I brought them together, for a discussion that was later published in the December 21, 2009, issue of *Le Nouvel Observateur*,[2] each of them had been taken severely to task by their most ardent supporters just for having agreed to meet with his opponent. Those supporters were quickly reassured, though, when the magazine came out and the dreaded "happy ending" was nowhere to be found. A tense, electric, and occasionally even violent atmosphere came across on the page. This was clearly no ordinary debate but rather a confrontation, almost in the physical sense implied by the word.

A second discussion nevertheless took place on February 16, 2010. In the meantime, there had been extremely heated, copious, indeed countless reader reactions to the first one. Dozens of websites and blogs had spread it around the Web, thousands of passionate comments had gone back and forth, and Éditions Lignes had quickly informed us of their interest in publishing

---

[2] Aude Lancelin, a journalist at the French weekly *Le Nouvel Observateur*, met with Badiou and Finkielkraut twice, in December 2009 and February 2010. This book is the revised and edited version of those discussions.

the text, augmented by the follow-up exchange.[3] The second session was nothing like the first. A somewhat artificial sort of nervous tension had abated. And yet the topics discussed, especially Israel, May '68, and the partial resurgence of the communist Idea, were anything but lightweight. One might even have legitimately expected a cataclysmic replay of the famous family dinner drawn by the political cartoonist Caran d'Ache in *Le Figaro* at the height of the Dreyfus Affair, with everyone fighting around the table and the caption below reading: "They talked about it – the Dreyfus Affair!" But no such thing happened, actually. Instead, there was genuine mutual curiosity this time around, and humor, too, which often punctuated their most difficult exchanges.

The debate was supposed to have lasted an hour and a half in mid-afternoon, but it stretched out to over four full hours. The winter sun had already disappeared from the place de la Bourse, but not the two opponents, who were still having at each other, recovering, and going at it again as night fell, while their horses had been dead for quite some time already, to parody Victor Hugo in *The Legend of the Centuries*. Blows – extremely hard ones at times – were dealt, points conceded, and even helping hands extended, but there was obviously no agreement about when an end should be called. Was one really necessary? This time, they had really entered the thick of the fray, with all that implies of unexpected areas of agreement, and insurmountable obstacles as well.

Neither of these men – for good reason – is known for his love of consensus and the middle ground, let alone for his tendency to compromise. This is in fact one of

---

[3] *L'Explication* (Paris: Lignes, 2010).

the few things they have in common, which also makes them stand out today. It's the same kind of integrity regarding what each thinks is the truth that needs to be told without pulling any punches. And it's also a proven courage, which has been tested since the mid-2000s in certain highly publicized intellectual controversies in which they have both at times been savagely attacked. Stick firmly to your position, whatever the cost, Alain Badiou would say. Don't be intimidated by the rumblings of political correctness, Alain Finkielkraut would reply. And then they'd quarrel over the nature of this hostility that must be relentlessly confronted.

But doesn't this mean that we should ask all the more insistently: "Why bother debating, then?" We should never engage in dialogue, either, if it's only a pretext for setting out side by side two diametrically opposed monologues or two self-centered viewpoints feigning ignorance of their hopeless symmetry and their unmistakable complicity in the farce of media manipulation. But such was not the case here either. Indeed, the chief interest of this book lies in demonstrating just that fact. Alain Finkielkraut is no more a typical neo-conservative than Alain Badiou is a knee-jerk progressive. If they were, it would be so easy for the proponents of worst-case politics [*la politique du pire*][4] and so convenient for all of those – and there are plenty of them – who would never give up an antagonism that excuses them from having to abandon their intellectual laziness and relinquish even a single one of their prejudices.

[4] The phrase "la politique du pire" refers to a deliberate strategy of allowing a situation to deteriorate to the point where some drastic action, whether revolutionary or counter-revolutionary, is required to change it.

Yet, since the 2007 presidential election and the stir caused by his book *The Meaning of Sarkozy*, Alain Badiou has been assigned the lead role of intransigent radical, battle-scarred yet fiendishly tenacious Maoist, and rabid pro-Palestinian activist, among other such shortcuts and falsifications that are always handy when it comes to imagining you can have access this way to a demanding body of work. But even a cursory reading of his recent politically interventionist books, not to mention his long-term philosophical work – recognized and studied worldwide since the publication of *Being and Event* in the late 1980s – would easily convince anyone of his exceedingly subtle, complex position. It is really only in France that the image of Alain Badiou as an extremist corrupter of innocent youth born after the fall of the Berlin Wall overshadows that of Badiou the philosopher of the One and the multiple, the subject of enormous conferences everywhere from Athens to Los Angeles.

Although he, too, is heavily caricatured, Alain Finkielkraut nevertheless stands out as a truly unique figure in the French landscape. I can attest all the more readily to this in that I happened to have clashed violently with him, on at least one occasion in the past, over the positions he took during the flare-up of violence in the French *banlieues* in 2005. A tireless opponent of a leveling, dominating mass democracy and a defender of a French public school system under threat from what he considers that mass democracy's inexorable expansion, the author of *The Defeat of the Mind*[5] has never in actual fact – a persistent myth

---

[5] *The Defeat of the Mind*, trans. Judith Friedlander (New York: Columbia University Press, 1995).

to the contrary notwithstanding – been part of the media-savvy syndicate called "the new philosophers." Although he fully shares their anti-Marxist sentiments and even co-founded the Institut d'études lévinassiennes with one of them, Bernard-Henri Lévy, Alain Finkielkraut has since that time taken his distance from the aggressively marketing aspect of their activity. Nor is there any trace in his career of support for America's wars in these early years of the twenty-first century. It would not even be going too far to say that his Péguyist defense of a vanishing eternal France, not to mention the unusual and, above all, very solitary support he has given a savagely pilloried writer such as Renaud Camus,[6] has made him a controversial figure even in the French neo-conservative movement, where he nonetheless has ardent supporters.

Even once these distortions have been corrected, though, the disagreement between the two parties is still very deep, and the gulf that had to be bridged in order for them to meet was as wide as could possibly be. Commenting on the growing resonance of Alain Badiou's thought in France, Alain Finkielkraut once characterized it, with alarm, as "the most violent philosophy there is," "a symptom of the return of radicality and of the collapse of anti-totalitarianism."[7] The Slovene philosopher Slavoj Žižek wrote a vigorous

---

[6] A prolific writer of nonfiction, social commentary, and novels, Renaud Camus ignited an enormous scandal in France in 2000 following the publication of *La Campagne de France*, his diary for 1994, which contained certain allegedly anti-Semitic statements. Finkielkraut, who shared some of his views on France and Israel, supported him throughout the controversy.

[7] Cited by Éric Aeschimann, "Mao en chaire," *Libération*, January 10, 2007, www.liberation.fr/grand-angle/2007/01/10/mao-en-chaire_81455.

theoretical response to this accusation in the French daily *Libération* when his very close fellow traveler's *Logics of Worlds*, the sequel to *Being and Event*, was published in March 2007. "As Badiou himself might put it in his unique Platonic way," he wrote, "true ideas are eternal, they are indestructible, they always return every time they are proclaimed dead."[8]

There is also no denying that, for some years now, Alain Badiou has been constantly on the attack against a strong intellectual trend that, in his view, has had a major impact on politics and in the media, with Alain Finkielkraut and Jean-Claude Milner generally considered to be among its foremost exponents in France. Alain Badiou usually describes this trend, which grew out of the former Maoist movement, as a vast, conservative counter-revolutionary movement, driven by, among other things, the symptomatic rejection of May '68 and the defense of a Christian and Jewish "West" allegedly under threat from the Islamist peril and its putative progressive accomplices, the successors to 1970s Third-Worldism. It is a dominant trend, which is also given to relentlessly invoking Stalinist and kindred crimes of the twentieth century in order to discredit any future attempts at political emancipation and blithely to succumb to the Right. The election of Nicolas Sarkozy in 2007, characterized by Badiou as "the advent of something disgusting, a blow against the symbolic structuring of French political life,"[9] was, in his view, both

---

[8] Slavoj Žižek, "Badiou pense à tout," *Libération*, March 22, 2007, www. liberation.fr/livres/2007/03/22/badiou-pense-a-tout_88141; Eng. trans. in *In Defense of Lost Causes* (London and New York: Verso, 2008), 4.

[9] Alain Badiou, *The Meaning of Sarkozy*, trans. David Fernbach (London and New York: Verso, 2008), 27.

the logical outcome and the high point of this trend.

The terrain was apparently not rough enough for the two men, so an even tougher issue had to be added to the mix. The question of Jewish identity, Saint Paul, and Israel would serve the purpose. When in 2005 Éditions Lignes brought out a collection of his texts (including some that were twenty years old) under the title *Circonstances 3: Portées du mot "juif"*[10], Alain Badiou had to contend with an extremely distressing campaign against him. Originally launched by *Les Temps modernes*, a journal whose editor, Claude Lanzmann, had admittedly been attacked by Cécile Winter in the book's appendix, the campaign was relentlessly propagated by a few malicious activists and aimed at nothing less than branding Badiou a far-left anti-Semite. And yet, right from the first pages of the book, Alain Badiou had spoken out with uncommon force about the emergence of a new anti-Semitism connected with the conflicts in the Middle East and their very real impact on certain Muslim minorities living in France: "[S]uffice it to say that the existence of this type of anti-Semitism is not in doubt, and the zeal with which some deny its existence – generally in the name of supporting the Palestinians or the working-class minorities in France – is extremely harmful," he wrote in no uncertain terms.[11] But when you want to demolish a thinker, there's no point in bothering to read him, is there?

---

[10] These essays were published together under the heading "Uses of the Word 'Jew'" as Part II of *Polemics*, trans. Steven Corcoran (London and New York: Verso, 2006). Inasmuch as *Polemics* also contains other, unrelated essays, the French edition will be cited below when necessary to avoid ambiguity.

[11] Badiou, *Polemics*, 158.

Alain Finkielkraut never took part, of course, in this concerted lynching. There was nevertheless a crucial basic disagreement between him and Badiou about the whole affair, having less to do, in fact – as you'll realize when you read this book – with the supposed philosophical anti-Judaism attributed to Badiou than with the very traditional question of the nation. The Jewish people's destinal singularity, Badiou has long claimed, is the injunction to universality, the call that historically and spiritually heralds the transcending of national affiliation. In this sense, he writes, it is "a glorious name of our history."[12] This vision is obviously disputed by Alain Finkielkraut. He, for his part, claims that identitarian rootedness is fully compatible with the dimension of universality, and he rejects even more emphatically the idea of abandoning the nation-state model, a model he considers as both unsurpassable and protective, particularly for a people who have been persecuted, as the Jewish people have been, throughout history.

As we know, this disagreement over the political significance of Judaism was in a way already present in latent form in the interviews given late in life by Jean-Paul Sartre to Benny Lévy and published in March 1980 in *Le Nouvel Observateur*, edited at the time by Jean Daniel and Claude Perdriel. The use Sartre wanted to make of the Jewish texts, which had just appeared in all their seductive force to Lévy, the former leader of the Gauche prolétarienne, was intended to rebuild the left, "that corpse lying on its back,"[13] under the

---

[12] Ibid., 167.
[13] Jean-Paul Sartre, *Situations*, trans. Benita Eisler (New York: George Braziller, 1965), 123.

horizon of a messianism with a universal vocation. Was Sartre fully aware that Benny Lévy, aged thirty-five at the time, was, on the contrary, going to draw on the study of Torah, the reading of Lévinas, and the "name 'Jew'" in general to bring about an anti-progressive shift in an increasingly large proportion of the French intelligentsia? Sartre and Lévinas are two major influences in the intellectual development and thought of Alain Badiou and Alain Finkielkraut respectively. They are two names that sound like two rallying names for two factions that, once again, rarely have anything to do with each other.

Will the insights afforded by this book help defuse the intense animosity that Badiou's and Finkielkraut's supporters often harbor toward one another? I obviously can't help but hope so, even if it would be quite naïve to think that clearing up misunderstandings in this way is all it would take for certain evil passions to subside. In the France of 2010, it is difficult still to be lulled into thinking that the Enlightenment ideal of providing a public forum for opposing viewpoints would suffice to calm people down and bring about perpetual peace. Well, "Hail to war!" then, as Proudhon said. Indeed, there is no reason to fear it, since it provides an opportunity to reawaken a French mode of thinking that increasingly seems to have given up on exerting any influence on the way things are in the world. Let us just hope that, when hostilities resume, the memory of the words shared in a spirit of camaraderie here will spare everyone any unnecessary wounds.

I
National Identity and Nations

Aude Lancelin: *A debate on "national identity" has been foisted on our country largely for electoral reasons. Predictably, it has quickly become heated. How should it be dealt with?*

Alain Finkielkraut: I don't know whether the debate is timely or not, but the concern is legitimate. In his famous 1882 lecture, Renan began by excluding any racial definition of the nation. "Human history is essentially different from zoology," he said, and he defined the nation as a spiritual principle, a soul (we shouldn't be afraid of that word), comprised of two components: a rich legacy of memories, a heritage of glory and regrets to share together, on the one hand, and, on the other, present-day consent, the desire to continue living together. Yet France today is in the grip of a twofold crisis, of heritage and consent. Hatred of France has become the order of the day among a significant fraction of the new French populations. You'd have to be out of touch with reality to think that this militant Francophobia is a response to state racism or the stigmatizing of foreigners. As for our heritage, our schools have been hard at work squandering it for forty years now. More and more French people, including the elites, are alienated from their own language, literature, history, and landscapes. It is because French civilization may be in the process of dying out that this national identity issue concerns so many people even though no one is fooled by the electoral ruse. The government can't be blamed for wanting to deal with the issue of national identity but rather for offloading responsibility for it onto a debate. I would have preferred a real cultural heritage transmission policy instead.

AL: *Yet the Sarkozy government's actions very often run counter to that discourse on transmission. Take, for example, its effort to eliminate the teaching of history to science-oriented students in the final year of high school* . . .

A. Finkielkraut: That's a contradiction. A choice has got to be made between Richard Descoings and Marc Bloch.[1] But educational reform along the latter lines

---

[1] Richard Descoings (1958–2012), for many years the director of the Institut des Études Politiques (Sciences Po), was a controversial figure. While he was applauded by some educational reformers, his efforts to bring more diversity into Sciences Po and, in particular, his introduction in 2001 of a program to recruit students from disadvantaged neighborhoods were the focus of bitter commentary by those who feared the devaluation of the elite school's demanding entrance requirements. Marc Bloch (1886–1944), one of the most influential historians of the twentieth century, was the co-founder of the Annales school of French social history. He famously defended French culture and values, remaining in France during World War II and fighting in the Resistance until he was captured, tortured, and shot by the Gestapo in 1944.

(recentering education around culture and restoring requirements) would bring middle- and high-school students, the teachers' unions, and the parents' associations out onto the streets to demonstrate. Cultural illiteracy for all is a victory of democracy that it will be very difficult to reverse.

Alain Badiou: A government-organized debate on "French identity" can only be an attempt to come up with administrative criteria to identify "who is a good French person and who isn't." The serious jurists of the Pétain government had worked very hard toward that end! They'd shown, with calm expertise, that Jews and other such aliens [*métèques*] were not good French people . . . So we can and should be very worried about the Sarkozy–Besson initiative. When the state starts being concerned about the legitimacy of people's identities, it can only mean we're in a period of darkest reaction, as historical experience has shown. This initiative is not just stupid and incoherent, then, as we see every day, but is also part and parcel of what I've called the Sarkozy government's "transcendental Pétainism." As soon as identity considerations are injected into politics or state power, we're dealing with a mentality that can only be called neo-fascist. This is because an identity-based definition of the population runs up against the fact that, since every population in the world today is composite, heterogeneous, and multi-faceted, the only reality such a definition can have will be a negative one. They won't succeed in defining "French civilization," a concept whose meaning completely escapes me; all they'll do is clearly designate those who aren't part of it. There are millions of people in our country who have been here, sometimes for decades, who have built our roads, our bridges, and our houses, who live in deplorable conditions, who have done all this for starvation wages, and whom, for the past thirty years, one administration after another has been hitting with persecutory laws, deporting, confining in no-law zones, monitoring, preventing from living with their families, and so on and so forth. We know in advance that these are the people who will be designated as not being really French. This political vision is absolutely abhorrent, and I'm weighing my words. Furthermore, I'm really surprised that the categories Alain Finkielkraut uses are the very traditional ones of reaction. The "heritage of the past" and "consent" are totally passive categories whose sole rationale is the imperative "family, homeland." This is a reactionary and conservative image of French identity. The heritage of France is a heritage that I am prepared to embrace when it's a matter of the French Revolution, the Commune, the universalism of the eighteenth century, the Resistance, or May '68. But it's a heritage I totally reject when it's a matter of the Restoration, the Versaillais,[2] colonialist and racist doctrines, Pétain, or Sarkozy. There's no such thing as "a" French heritage. Rather, there is a constitutive division of that heritage between what's acceptable in terms of a minimal universalism and what should be rejected precisely because, in France, it has to do with the extreme ferocity of the possessing classes and with the monopolizing of the idea of "national identity" by an oligarchy of

---

[2] The Versaillais were the counter-revolutionary forces whose slaughter of tens of thousands of Communards in May 1871 led to the defeat of the Paris Commune.

careerists, politicians, military men, and media lackeys. People – and Alain Finkielkraut in particular – are always talking about the blood that other people, the "totalitarians," as he calls them, have on their hands. But "national identity" has actually provided the most egregious examples of this. You'd have to look long and hard to find another wholesale slaughter as senseless and horrific as that of World War I. Yet it was strictly connected to national identity: that's what people were taken in by. It's very clear that national identity, when it refers to undivided memory and hereditary and familial consent, is nothing but the return to the tired old categories of tradition and leads only to war, against the "bad French" on the domestic front and against "the others" on the foreign front. The public debate today is between two disastrous positions: on the one side, free-market consensus and universal commercialism and, on the other, the retreat into identities, which is a reactionary and, moreover, totally ineffective defense against that globalization.

A. Finkielkraut: It's true that it's possible to have a racial and deterministic conception of national identity and treat it as a fixed, biologically transmitted trait, but it was precisely *against* such an idea that the president of the Republic's speech at La Chapelle-en-Vercors was directed. There is a debate, he said, but race cannot be part of it: "We are French because we don't see ourselves as a single race, because we don't allow ourselves to be confined to a single origin or to a single religion."[3] It is

---

[3] Speech by Nicolas Sarkozy, La Chapelle-en-Vercors, November 12, 2009, www.ambafrance-uk.org/President-Sarkozy-s-La-Chapelle-en.

legitimate and even necessary to point up the contradiction between the proclaimed desire to safeguard national identity and a policy of abandoning our heritage. But why is there such deafness? Why denounce as racist a speech so obviously anti-racial? Because, in the eyes of the prevailing anti-racism and anti-fascism, national identity itself, whatever its definition, is "repulsive" – or "abhorrent," to use Alain Badiou's word. So that means that our task would have to be to eliminate all identity predicates – disaffiliation, in other words. In order to be ourselves – that is, faithful to our universal vocation – all our distinguishing features would have to be wiped out. In order not to exclude anyone, we'd have to empty ourselves out, rid ourselves of all substance, and be nothing, ultimately, but the gesture itself of openness.

AL: *There are the words of the president of the Republic, which are those of a party leader during an electoral campaign, and then there's the reality of the debate in which, clearly, suspects are being named, and you know very well who they are . . .*

A. Finkielkraut: Simply to brush off as unimportant the demonstrations celebrating Algeria's victory over Egypt eight years after the booing of "La Marseillaise" at the France–Algeria match[4] is, as Arthur Koestler said about the communists, like having "the eyes to see and a mind conditioned to explain away what they saw."[5] Let me

---

[4] In October 2001, the French national anthem was booed at a soccer match between France and Algeria at the Stade de France by French-born youth of immigrant background.

[5] Arthur Koestler, *The Ghost in the Machine* (London: Hutchinson, 1967), 262.

also remind you that family reunification legislation was introduced back in 1974. What really bothers me about this hyperbolism is that it no longer makes any distinction between Marc Bloch and Pétain, between Péguy and Drumont,[6] between Bernanos[7] and Brasillach,[8] or between the nation according to De Gaulle and the *Volk* according to Hitler. Most of the Resistance fighters referred to the indivisible national heritage to justify their resistance, and what did Simone Weil say? That there was no more hideous spectacle than that of a people no longer attached to anything, with no fidelity whatsoever.[9]

A. Badiou: But fidelity to what?

A. Finkielkraut: To the Coronation Rite of Reims and to the Fête de la Fédération,[10] to "the Republic one and indivisible, our kingdom of France" . . . [11]

---

[6] The notorious anti-Semite Édouard Drumont (1844–1917) was the author, in particular, of *La France Juive* (1886), which portrayed a France under the domination of the Jews and argued for their exclusion from society.

[7] The Catholic writer Georges Bernanos (1888–1948) was the author of a number of highly regarded novels, including his masterpiece, *Diary of a Country Priest*. Originally a monarchist and outspoken partisan of right-wing politics, he gradually became disillusioned with fascism and was a strong supporter of De Gaulle in World War II.

[8] Robert Brasillach (1909–1945), a gifted novelist and critic, was the editor of the rabidly anti-Semitic, fascist weekly *Je suis partout*. He was executed after World War II for the "intellectual crimes" of advocating collaborationism, denunciation, and incitement to murder.

[9] Simone Weil, *The Need for Roots*, trans. Arthur Wills (New York: Harper Collins, 1977), 109.

[10] The Fête de la Fédération in 1790 celebrated the first anniversary of the storming of the Bastille and the short-lived constitutional monarchy.

[11] This phrase of Charles Péguy's elsewhere elicited Finkielkraut's comment "So the Republic is part of the very tradition it combats . . .," in Alain Finkielkraut and Edwy Plenel, *La Nation à l'épreuve* (Paris: Éditions du Tricorne, 2002), 42.

A. Badiou: Of course, of course, but careful . . . There are a huge number of people in this country who are faithful to a lot of other things and first of all to passing down their property through inheritance, as has been the case since the dawn of time. They are faithful to the sequences of history in which the popular forces were thrown into disarray. Even as regards the Resistance itself they deliberately ignore the ultimately key role, like it or not, played by the communist armed forces. Taken in isolation, "heritage" and "fidelity" are meaningless. What we should ask is: Whose heritage? Fidelity to what? In fact, you presume – and that's why your approach is absolutely tautological – that the problem of national identity has already been resolved. It's to this undivided but non-existent identity that you say we have to be faithful. I myself am faithful in as exemplary a manner as possible to revolutionary France, to its paradigmatic universality, to the 1793 constitution, which declared that, whenever a man took in and raised an orphan, anywhere in the world, well, just by doing so he acquired French nationality. I'm all for an across-the-board, immediately transmissible identity of that sort. But I don't know of any example where the inclusion of a figure of identity in the conception of the state can be considered as progressive, in any way, shape, or form. The question of involvement in the Resistance went far beyond the question of the liberation of the country, as you are well aware, and had nothing to do with a national "identity." The most combative armed Resistance groups in France were made up of communists who came from all over Europe and whom Pétain, in the name of French identity, accused of being traitors, which really takes the cake! When Aragon wrote "My

8

Party has restored to me the colors of France,"[12] both aspects should be emphasized: France, of course, but also the Party, which was for him the name of the internationalist and communist vision.

A. Finkielkraut: If an inventory has to be drawn up, we should start by making one of communism, too . . . All one does by discrediting or aggressively breaking down the desire for French civilization to continue is embrace the current trend toward world music, world cuisine, planetary civilization, and the global village. Characterizing this surrender to the trend we're being swept away by as "resistance" to Sarkozy is going a bit far.

AL: *But isn't Sarkozyism itself part of that trend?*

A. Finkielkraut: That's exactly what I have against it.

A. Badiou: Your philosophical and political categories lock you into an extremely narrow conception of the question. You're caught between consenting to universal commodification, to the dilution of everything into the global village, on the one hand, and a theory of identity that is supposedly the one and only defense against it, on the other. It's exactly as if Marx in 1848 had said that the only alternatives were global capitalism or French nationalism. But in actual fact Marx, a century and a half ago, defined a form of political

---

[12] Louis Aragon, "From the Poet to his Party," in *Defeat and Beyond: An Anthology of French Wartime Writing (1940–1945)*, ed. Germaine Brée and George Bernauer (New York: Pantheon, 1970), 248.

internationalism that's not reducible to either one. And that's what our problem is today. It's not about clutching onto so-called identities that we draw from tradition and think should be restored in order to mount an illusory resistance to the immense power of universal commodification. Rather, the problem is about finding a way that involves neither the supremacy of capital and its "democratic" mumbo-jumbo nor the frenzied manufacturing of domestic enemies who are supposedly undermining our "identity." And in this regard I am committed to the only tradition that was founded in just such a way and that refused to be co-opted by diehard nationalism in the nineteenth century, namely, the revolutionary internationalist tradition. It's the only one. That's moreover why it was the hard kernel of the resistance to identitarian fascism everywhere, and especially in France.

AL: *Do you in fact think, as Alain Badiou claims you do, that identity attribution is the only option we have for resisting this uniform planetary commodification that you, too, denounce, although from a very different perspective?*

A. Finkielkraut: I deplore the loss of things, but French civilization isn't the only thing that might be lost. I'm also concerned about the destruction of the earth, creeping ugliness, the decrease in attention span, the demise of silence, and our move into the technological age in which everything is being degraded. And for just this reason I think that, to confront a disaster like this, we can't be satisfied with a politics of liberation. We also need a politics of responsibility. What bothers me about

Alain Badiou's conception of politics is that there's no place in it for gratitude, for fidelity, for what Hannah Arendt called the love for the world. That's the philosophical and existential perspective from which I see things, and, in an even more general way, I'm struck by the critical poverty of the critique of domination.

AL: *What do you have in mind? What current of thought or ideas, exactly?*

A. Finkielkraut: All of them. The model in which the world is divided into the dominant and the dominated, a model that's so deeply ingrained that nobody protests when a decision of the European Court requires crucifixes to be removed from Italian schools, while the Swiss decision not to allow any more minarets to be built is treated as a disgrace by a quasi-unanimous press. Crucifixes today, even deactivated ones (public school in Italy is secular), are perceived as emblems of domination, while people see in the minaret the rallying sign of the oppressed, the banner of the wretched of the earth. We're constantly being brought back to this big division.

A. Badiou: Those are trivial issues; that's how I feel about it. I'm a strict Nietzschean when it comes to issues like these. God is dead, and has been for a long time. So we need to begin with the idea that, when we're dealing with so-called phenomena of civilization or religion, they're hiding something and are other than what they seem. What's really behind them? We don't see any mystical figures, deep religious thinkers, innovative theology, and so on. We see nothing of the sort. What we do see are organized agitators, anonymous attacks, totally stereotypical rhetoric. So what is the political figure hiding behind this rhetoric of radical Islamism? In any case, when it comes to being identitarian, it sure as hell is! And you'd want to imitate it, you'd want to fight it with a quasi-desperate defense of "Western civilization" or "French identity," which is being invaded and threatened by the barbarians . . .

A. Finkielkraut: No, I don't!

A. Badiou: Yes, you do! Don't try to evade the consequences of your identitarian stance! When you see young people screaming their support for Algeria, they're anti-French barbarians, in your opinion. In my opinion, they're no more so than were the Tyrosse rugby club fans in the Landes region fifty years ago when they screamed at the Paris Racing Club fans. It's just the shabby imaginary of the identity conflict, for which sports serves as a well-known outlet. The latest wave of immigrants always remain attached to their past, which is only natural. Already in the nineteenth century people were accusing the proletarians of Paris of being Auvergnat illiterates before driving them out and killing them in June 1848. There's nothing new about any of this. When I was a child in Toulouse, people used to snicker about the Spanish Civil War refugees and say that they put coal in their bathtubs. It's dismaying to see you doing the same thing! The general proletarization of the world has spread beyond our continent: that's the only new phenomenon. First we had the Auvergnats, the Italians, and the Poles; now we have the Sri Lankans and the Malians. And you think that *that's* the problem "French" thought should be focused on? Just between us, with the world everywhere under the control of an extremely close-knit network of financial and media oligarchies that impose a rigid model of development and do so at the price of crises and never-ending wars, to think that the problem, in such a world, is whether girls should wear a headscarf or not strikes me as truly preposterous. And so I see that as a bad omen. It's the start of a creeping stigmatization targeting one particular minority. And beware that this stigmatization, under the pretext of national identity, of values that must be preserved, and so forth, doesn't then spread throughout the country in uncontrollable ways. The vote against the minarets by millions of idiotic Swiss is just one episode in this trend, and you're responsible for it. Clearly, the intellectuals and "feminists" who made a big fuss over the headscarf twenty years ago are responsible for the minaret phenomena now, and will be responsible for even worse tomorrow. You want an ethics of responsibility? Well, take responsibility! The intellectuals are the ones who started this whole thing . . .

A. Finkielkraut: Régis Debray, Élisabeth de Fontenay, Élisabeth Badinter, Catherine Kintzler, and me . . .

A. Badiou: That list is incomplete, albeit accurate. Well, it's a heavy responsibility. I also have some long-time female friends who were glad the Americans were bombing Kabul because it was for the cause of women's liberation. You can have fun, can't you, tossing things like that around here and there, like mere identity provocations, but then they spread, they take hold of people and become a crude and simplistic view according to which we're really good and those other people are really bad. And they'll be described increasingly systematically in those terms. And, year after year, laws that are increasingly segregationist and discriminatory will be passed. In all these civilizational matters a machine enabling identity to be injected into politics will be set in motion, and you will certainly not be able to control it. Others will.

A. Finkielkraut: We're being led to believe that the French today are obsessed with hatred of the other, rejection of the other ... Let me remind you, though, that French schools don't exclude anyone; they exclude the headscarf, which is something completely different. Let me remind you that, if there's any fear today, it's not fear of foreigners; it's fear of the hatred that some immigrants or children of immigrants feel toward us, which has no precedent in the previous waves of immigration. It's not a matter of responding to this hatred with stigmatization but rather of saying that there are rules, values, and traditions that are non-negotiable in France. The beauty of the world is also its diversity. The ultra-liberals want a smooth world, without signs of particularity and without identity communities; they want France to be nothing but one big train station waiting room, a random collection of individuals bustling around – but is that what *we* want? Do we want mobility to be people's last word and dying breath? So there you have it. That's all I'm trying to say.

AL: *Everyone knows the ancient precept: "When in Rome, do as the Romans do." But those people, the* *people from the poor suburban neighborhoods, don't live in Rome. Very specifically, they live in completely neglected neighborhoods and so their access to French citizenship is still pretty largely theoretical.*

A. Finkielkraut: First of all, things are never that simple. The phenomena of demographic substitution, in spite of what some people would have us believe, are not due to the stigmatization of foreigners. If you live in Bobigny and have to drive to find a non-halal butcher shop, you'll move. That's the situation. My second response is that, for you, Alain Badiou, there is no legitimate politics except through the affirmation of equality. But something else has to be added (and here's where the idea of heritage begins to take shape): we're the heirs of a tradition of gallantry, which is to say of a certain kind of coexistence based on the mixing of the sexes. But the veil imposes separation and in so doing reduces women to the status of sexual objects. In Algerian Arabic, a woman without a veil is said to be naked. She can be either lascivious or covered up: those are the only alternatives. She is, at any rate from the point of view of *our* civilization, obscene.

A. Badiou: If we have to choose between waiting rooms, it's important to see that yours leaves at large a rapacious oligarchy of predators that's in control of the waiting room. I'd like for that oligarchy, the secret, global instigator of everything going on, to be attacked first in your discourse, rather than the farmer who has just arrived in France because he couldn't support his family back home and so it's both a necessity and a duty for him to go wherever he can find the means to survive, just as millions of French farmers who left their farms for the city did before him. He's a proletarian, in a nutshell. I'm fond of that old word. There has to be a hierarchy of importance, after all! It's more important to attack the nucleus of power today than to spend all your time attacking the proletarians, on the typical reactionary pretext that, since they come from somewhere else, they still have the trappings of that otherness about them. Given the way they're treated, it's quite understandable that they're not overflowing with love for this country. I myself am happy to love France but only for what's lovable about it. I, too, hate the current forms of power in France, the ones that are now in control of its future as a nation.

When you say that these people hate us, who or what do they hate? They don't hate France: that's totally wrong, trust me. I was involved in politics with them for decades. I'd be more inclined to think that they're the last true patriots, because they still believe in a democratic and revolutionary France; they're still shocked and deeply hurt by the fact that they're persecuted. At bottom, they're patriots, Alain Finkielkraut, because they hope that the current hostile, identity discourse is not what France is really all about. The only thing they hate about France is what they perceive as protocols of stigmatization. It's France as it comes across in your narrow-minded identity discourse that they dislike. It has to be said that that France has never looked too good, either now or in the past.

A. Finkielkraut: Maybe there's a real divide between us on the question of hatred. In a 1945 lecture organized by Amitié française, Camus said in substance: Nazism forced us to hate, but now it is essential to overcome hatred and never let criticism descend to the level of insult. He called this "remaking our political mentality."[13] At the same time, René Char formulated the same recommendation: "After the fire, we are in favor of erasing the traces and sealing up the labyrinth. An exceptional climate cannot be prolonged."[14] Sartre made the opposite decision. He wanted to prolong the exceptional climate of the Resistance by turning politics into the continuation of absolute war, and so he wrote: "All the value that an oppressed man can still have in his own eyes, he puts into the hatred that he bears other men."[15] Camus is renowned today, but Sartre is actually the big winner. Hatred isn't rejected, it's indulged in, and the *reductio ad hitlerum* is going full blast. When you compare Sarkozy to Pétain, as you do, Alain Badiou, or when you claim, along with the Médiapart website and 40,000 angry citizens, that "for the first time since 1944–5 the ideology of the far right – that simultaneously Maurrassian, Orleanist, and elitist right that never accepted liberal democracy and, with the collapse of the Republic in 1940, experienced its divine surprise[16] – is being expressed at the highest echelons of the Republic,"[17] then you're not being clear-sighted, let alone courageous. You're adopting an intellectually

---

[13] Albert Camus, *Resistance, Rebellion and Death: Essays*, trans. Justin O'Brian (New York: Vintage, 1995), 59.

[14] René Char, "Lettre à Francis Curel," in *Œuvres complètes* (Paris: Gallimard, 1983), 637.

[15] Jean-Paul Sartre, "Reply to Albert Camus," in *Situations*, trans. Benita Eisler (New York: Georges Braziller, 1965), 99–100.

[16] In 1941 Charles Maurras acclaimed the advent of Pétain's Vichy regime as a "divine surprise."

[17] Edwy Plenel's article "Une honte nationale," from which this citation is drawn, appeared on the Médiapart website on December 8, 2009. It is accessible at http://lepartidegauche26.over-blog.com/article-une-honte-nationale-edwy-plenel-mediapart-40933213.html.

comfortable and psychologically gratifying position. In a context like that, everything's simple. You never have to deal with dilemmas or problems, you can simply ignore the conflicts of duties, and you can indulge in easy outrage because the only people you ever encounter are scoundrels. "A rapacious oligarchy," you say, Alain Badiou, but one that nevertheless imposes a progressive income tax and makes the richest citizens pay 50 percent of their earnings.

A. Badiou: But don't forget the history of that income tax ... and the incredible popular battles that were responsible for getting it enacted! The people who fought to get it enacted fought against enemies. You can't make the category of enemy disappear; you simply can't. And you can't make a mistake about who the enemy is either: it's Sarkozy and his cohorts rather than the young people in the *banlieue*.

A. Finkielkraut: The young people in the *banlieue* aren't my enemies. They've never been, Alain Badiou, I swear. On the contrary, when I say that rules have to be established, I think that I'm reaching out to them and that showing them a flattering and pleasing image of themselves is, on the contrary, abandoning them to their plight.

A. Badiou: A lot of good your reaching out to them does ... A positive, universal destiny for these young people would be to organize themselves with the aim of destroying the established order – *that* would be an ideal positive solution. All you're suggesting to them is that they become society's obedient lapdogs.

A. Finkielkraut: It's your radicalism that's doing them in. It's your raised fist that's dooming them. By offering them destruction or submission as the only alternatives you're not helping them; you're blocking all other possible options. And this brings me to the psychological benefit of the eternal analogy with the dark years of the war. If Sarkozy is Pétain, then that makes *you* a member of the Resistance. I urge you, you and the intellectual left, which, under your auspices, is becoming completely megalomaniacal, to stop kidding yourselves. Sarkozy isn't a leader, he's a target. Insulting the president of the Republic has become the most widespread, popular pastime on the Net and in the media. When the political authorities were strong, there was an obsequious conformism; now, though, those authorities are weak and there's a sarcastic conformism.

A. Badiou: You have a consensual-type basic axiom: living together. You act as if we were living under conditions where there was no real enemy and we'd necessarily have respectful relations with the highest echelons of the Republic. You describe a virtual political scene that has nothing whatsoever to do with the real scene. In the real scene, there are enemies, power grabbers, enormous inequalities, and a whole stratum of society that's discriminated against by the law itself. There are rules, contrary to what you say, but they are unilateral ones. And, in a situation like this, you seem to think that what should demand philosophers' attention is the provincial enthusiasm – so common in sports – of a second generation of Algerian immigrants for the victory of their country of origin's team. All you talk about are trivial issues, and the way you talk about them is all the more dangerous in that you invest a sort of totally excessive affect in them. I wish you'd direct that over-the-top affect toward the *real* enemies.

A. Finkielkraut: You have such an imperious idea of the real that you declare any phenomenon that might contradict it null and void. If it doesn't want to be invalidated, it had better behave – i.e., conform to your system. For you, the only factual truth is a truth validated by class struggle. But the undermining of educational curricula is not a trivial matter. The frequent physical attacks on teachers aren't a trivial matter, any more than is the contempt for these teachers because they earn only 1,500 euros a month. So you and I don't have the same view of things. But I'm absolutely not making a case here for consensus; I'm fighting against the Resistance-type megalomania I mentioned a moment ago and for civil dissensus. The question I ask myself when I listen to and read you, Alain Badiou, is: Is there any place for a legitimate adversary? In the heat of battle, the adversary isn't legitimate; it's evil and must be combatted and destroyed. And once the adversary has been destroyed? Then it's a happily-ever-after fairytale, a Hallelujah without end. Communist politics is ruthless, and its utopia is pure kitsch. It replaces the Greek ideal of friendship – the dialogue about the world – with fraternity, which is to say the transparency of hearts, the fusion of minds.

A. Badiou: No, that's a joke . . . What a caricature! Any schoolchild knows that Marxists make a distinction between antagonistic contradictions, with the enemy, and non-antagonistic contradictions, which are also known as "contradictions among the people." It's the latter that are more important in politics because the unity and, thus, the discipline and power of collective self-affirmation are dependent on them. These contradictions can be very sharp, but they absolutely must be handled by discussion, backed up by facts. And they'll go on existing forever. That's the whole meaning of what, in your own jargon, you call "civil dissensus." I get the feeling that you're making yourself seem more ignorant about all these issues than you really are.

AL: *Alain Badiou, you've often said that that power you were talking about ought to be defeated by "the street" rather than by the ballot box. It seems as if you're making these young people of immigrant background the leading edge of the emancipatory movement you advocate, just as you're fighting for the revival of the communist project. This is a vision that sets you in radical opposition to Alain Finkielkraut, who, for his part, fears that the lessons of the twentieth century will be forgotten and the gains made by the anti-totalitarian movement lost . . .*

A. Badiou: I regard the current leaders the way Marx regarded the leaders in 1848: they're "agents of capital." That's what they have increasingly emphatically become again since the 1980s, assisted in this by the ideological counter-revolution in which Alain Finkielkraut, along with others, has actively participated. It has consisted in: (1) discrediting every form of the communist hypothesis and (2) relegitimizing parliamentary democracy as the unsurpassable horizon of politics. Here's my position. Like everyone else, I can assess the disastrous outcome of the state communisms of the twentieth century. What's more, I can do so better than you, Alain Finkielkraut, because I know their most appalling details, and the question of communism is the question that concerns me most deeply. But that is in no way a reason to tolerate things as they are. So there are enemies, to whom I grant no legitimacy. Consequently, we need to build an ideological, political force whose nature, for the time being, is completely unclear. At any rate, it will necessarily have to be an international force – as Marx perfectly saw, moreover. Capitalist and imperialist violence has led to the fact that there is only one world. Where people come from is ultimately much less important than the values, organizations, and worldviews they'll choose. Emancipation, or its fundamental core, presupposes equality and hence the struggle against the total social dominance of private property. I, too, when all is said and done, am proposing a sort of rule to these "young people": the rule of political discipline. We're unfortunately still a long way today from there being any political discipline of the poorest, of the disadvantaged. Building a new discipline is the problem of our times. And it won't be accomplished through school or any of the state institutions. The school system is done for, as is most of the legacy of the Third and Fourth Republics. Everything needs to be done on a grand scale, independently of these relics that an increasingly tense melancholy makes you cling to.

A. Finkielkraut: I have in fact tried to learn as much as possible from the experience of totalitarianism. The Polish philosopher Leszek Kołakowski has helped me with this: "[t]he essential quality of the Stalinist era" was "the imposition of a single alternative on human reality in all spheres of social life."[18] We have to get away from all that. Badiou's world consists of two camps, two blocs, two forces, and then only "one," once victory has been achieved. There's never any place for plurality in this supposedly progressive vision of the world.

A. Badiou: Given that my entire philosophical oeuvre consists in elaborating an ontology of the multiple and that one of its essential propositions is "The One does not exist," I'd have to be pretty illogical to be opposed to plurality! You're the one who doesn't want any plurality, because it scares the hell out of you . . .

A. Finkielkraut: I'm not what your system would like to make me out to be, namely, a defender of the way things are. I see this world turning into a non-world and my heart aches for it, as did Lévi-Strauss's, but that sadness doesn't make me a counter-revolutionary.

A. Badiou: It's very clear to me that the basic subjective feature in your case is a kind of melancholy. I find it touching, because I can share it in a way. It would be hard to find someone more profoundly French than I am. One of the first sentences in my book *Theory of the Subject*[19] is "I love my country, France." You and I could relate to each other about a certain image of old French charm and lament that vanished charm together melancholically. The only problem is that, in your case,

18 Leszek Kołakowski, *Toward a Marxist Humanism*, trans. J. Z. Peel (New York: Grove Press, 1969), 100.
19 Alain Badiou, *Theory of the Subject*, trans. Bruno Bosteels (London and New York: Continuum, 2005).

the melancholy turns aggressive and dreams of segrega-tions, prohibitions, and uniformity. And that tendency leads you to regard new, irreversible phenomena as dan-gerous or harmful, whereas they're just the historical life of things. Let's accept once and for all, I repeat, that the massive arrival of people from Africa is the continua-tion of the process that began in the nineteenth century when the Auvergnats and Savoyards came to Paris, and then the Poles went to cities in the north of France and the Italians to Marseille. Without this kind of broad view of things, the image one has of France will be narrow-minded and dangerous. The only vision that can give meaning to the word "France" is what constitutes French universalism in the eyes of the whole world, namely, the relationship with the French Revolution, with popular politics. Yes, *that*, on the contrary, at least on the subjective level, can be salutary.

A. Finkielkraut: A high-school teacher was presented with a petition from her final-year students putting her on notice either to leave or to change her attitude because she'd been so authoritarian as to forbid the use of cell phones in class! "Get lost or get with it!" this col-lective letter essentially said. "Don't be difficult. Just get with the program. Let communication flourish and stop cultural transmission, once and for all, from bugging the hell out of everyone." We're depriving the newcomers to the world, at their request, of a basic right, the right to continuity. I note this change, I speak out to combat it, but I haven't the slightest hope of winning the battle.

AL: *Alain Badiou, your position is characterized by a radical universalism, a reasoned refusal to allow any* *communitarian attribution to play a determining role in political matters. This is without a doubt one of the issues on which you are furthest apart from Alain Finkielkraut, who seems to make a distinction, moreover, between the current wave of immigration and the earlier ones. Would you care to say a bit more about this disagreement between the two of you?*

A. Finkielkraut: When we reflect on such sensitive issues we should constantly be careful not to let the consideration of laws or general tendencies blunt our sensitivity to specific situations. People aren't mere sociological samples: that's the main thing we've learned from anti-racism. I nevertheless think, as opposed to Alain Badiou, that there's a profound difference between the earlier waves of immigration and today's. An activist of AC Le Feu [Association Collectif Liberté, Égalité, Fraternité, Ensemble, Unis], an organization established after the 2005 riots, stated: "I'm not a French citizen of immigrant background, I'm a French citizen who's part of French diversity" – which means that the France within him is just himself. He makes demands and has claims to put forward but no debt to settle or even just to acknowledge. "Thanks" is a word that never crosses his lips. He owes nothing to the country he lives in. The notion of diversity relieves him of the dual burden of republican citizenship and French civilization. This reminded me of my own situation, since I, too, am a French citizen of immigrant background. My father arrived in France in the late 1920s, my mother in 1948. They are both survivors. My paternal grandparents were deported from Bordeaux after being denounced by a smuggler. My father was also deported. The quarrel with France in my family was a very fraught one. My parents felt somewhat aloof. And yet I could never make such a statement about myself, because the France within me is not just myself. France is something that was shared with me. It offered itself to me – and this is its greatness – as an adoptive country. France is a language I grew up with, a culture that I (partly) appropriated, a heritage that was passed down to me through school. With the recent, very vocal promotion of the theme of diversity it's a whole new ball-game. This new social norm makes for a France in which people's origins count only if they're foreign and in which all identities (religious, ethnic, regional, or sexual) are welcome, except French identity. Yet a nation that recognizes itself only in the diversity of its various components is no longer a historical subject but a sociological object, and it is sheer absurdity on the government's part to try, as it is doing, to have it both ways. I believe deeply that France should not be a sort of potluck dinner to which everyone contributes their own dish. What I feel is a compassionate patriotism or, as Simone Weil put it, affection for a beautiful, precious, and perishable thing. And I wish more people shared that feeling.

A. Badiou: Let me repeat: I love my country, France; I take full responsibility for that sentence. But even though I can understand your compassionate patriotism, I would unhesitatingly oppose my own constructive patriotism to it. To your affection for particular features I would oppose my enthusiasm for the unconditional gifts that France is capable of giving all of humanity. The France of the ideals of the Revolution, or the France of the Resistance, or of the Paris Commune, but also the France of Corneille's plays or Proust's novels, is worthy of my love only to the extent that I know that this France is addressed to everyone and is worthy of everyone's love. And that's why such a love not only doesn't contradict but actually *requires* the maxim: "The proletariat has no country." The only science is the science that can be transmitted to all countries; the only poems are the poems that are in dialogue with those of every language, through time and space. So it's only normal that there can be no creative new politics capable of shattering inegalitarian, communitarian figures except on the scale of the whole world. Marx already considered the nation-state framework to be obsolete. The historical reality of the high point of French nationalism was World War I. Millions died for no reason whatsoever. France is worthy of making a gift of itself to newcomers only to the extent that it has been the France that was capable of welcoming them with its policy. The France that doesn't welcome them, that passes law after law discriminating against them, is quite simply the France of World War I or the France of Pétain – in other words, the France that locks people out and has no protocol of existence other than its closure. And *you* say "no potluck dinner." But you've got to see what that means concretely for the people who are going to come here. It means detention camps, police persecution, and constant screening of people who are not Islamic radicals but simply people from here, people on the same difficult, tortuous, repressive journey as their predecessors who came to the cities from the country. Say or do what you will, you're in favor of designating those people as suspects. And to me that's outrageous. Today, more than ever, we need to think outside the nation-state box. So that means diversity! But everything is diverse; everything has always been made up of absolutely stupendous differences. France itself, under Louis XIV, wasn't even linguistically unified. So this opposition between the unity and diversity of France is total bullshit. France is made up of a million different things, so why should it suddenly say: "No, we've got to draw a line somewhere! *This* type of difference, the Muslim one, for example, is no good." Those are ultimately police and persecution methods. Either fetishism of the nation or communitarianism: once again, I note that you're locking yourself into a narrow alternative. But there's another hypothesis. The real future construction is a totally internationalist vision of the figure of politics. And to be able to build internationalism within the country is a boon, not a bane.

AL: *And yet, up till now, we haven't come up with anything other than the nation-state framework to impose wealth redistribution via the income tax, the social safety net, and other achievements that incidentally, you yourself, Alain Badiou, defend. With all due respect to alter-globalists à la Toni Negri, who are even calling for an unlikely "global minimum wage," all of this has been made possible only by our relying on the nation-state framework. . .*

A. Badiou: But that's all just temporary! It has absolutely never been proved, nor can it ever be, that this is the only possible framework.

AL: *But that's because you don't take finitude into account, or rather, as a good revolutionary, you decide never to take it into account – as opposed to Jean-Jacques Rousseau, moreover, an author I understand* *is particularly close to your heart, who thought that a nation that was too extensive was doomed to disappear . . .*

A. Badiou: Perhaps. That *is* kind of true. My position could in fact be described as a Rousseauism of the infinite.

A. Finkielkraut: Using the word "persecution" to describe current immigration policy strikes me as a total exaggeration . . . European politicians are torn by conflicting demands.

A. Badiou: Well, that's because you don't know the people who are its victims. Let me tell you something: you're talking about things from a distance.

A. Finkielkraut: Our continent could hardly be described as a fortress. So hospitality . . .

A. Badiou: Sorry, but you can't call having people come here because we need them "hospitality"! Having them come here to slave away in the restaurant industry or dig holes in the sidewalk for starvation wages is a very odd notion of hospitality.

A. Finkielkraut: And the need to preserve the welfare state's achievements . . . If we lived under a free-market regime, the movement of people would be a lot easier to ensure. To welcome is to give something, and to give something there has to be something to give and someone to be receptive. And I've been observing the gradual disappearance of receptivity of that sort.

A. Badiou: You're talking about something you don't know anything about. The overwhelming majority of those people have come here to work like dogs, but not on account of France's great benevolent hospitality ... They've come to dig our ditches and clean up our shit – and do it for less than the minimum wage, while our famous "welfare state" doesn't apply to them because we refuse to give them legal documentation. They can't even get proper treatment in hospitals. And these are the people you blame for the deterioration of French identity?

A. Finkielkraut: That's a very vivid picture you've painted, but you're overlooking one huge fact: since the late 1970s, family flows, not labor flows, have been the main vector of immigration. And you're accusing me unfairly: I don't blame anyone for the *deterioration* of French identity; I'm just shocked to see the growing *aversion* to that identity. In an article in *Le Monde*, a newspaper as careful as they come to avoid any stigmatization, the mayor of Cavaillon, a town where there's endemic violence, was quoted as saying that municipal workers had had garbage thrown on them from a housing project building, to shouts of: "Keep cleaning up our shit, you fucking French!"

A. Badiou: Well, of course! The good, white, well-integrated French have tons of stories like that about the Africans or Algerians, just as they used to have about the Jews or the "Levantines." What truth is there to them? What importance do they have? The Swiss who voted against the minarets have never seen an Arab in their entire lives. That whole affair was an ideological construction. You're constructing the Muslims ideologically the way the Jews were constructed in the 1930s. That's what you're doing, with the same slurs: they're people who aren't really part of our country, who privately or publicly hate us, who are a closed community, who refuse to be integrated into the French state, and so on. And you think you can do so with impunity? Well, you're wrong. There will be people who'll exploit that pseudo-intellectual construction. Because the situation is serious. But not in the way you think it is. It's not French identity that's under threat; French identity has seen a lot worse. What's under threat is the minimum level of internal and popular cohesion necessary to keep all this from ending up some day with dark forces being absolutely dominant. I'm well aware that you, Alain Finkielkraut, won't side with those forces, but you'll be partly responsible for them. Identity designations of that sort can't be introduced into politics without there being extremely serious consequences. You're perfectly aware of that. There's no "immigrant problem" in France, there's no "Muslim problem," any more than there was a "Jewish problem" in the 1930s. Why are you using your intelligence and talent to contribute to the absolutely fantastical construction of this sort of "problem" from incidents that can always be dug up, if not simply fabricated? The anti-Semites also dug up "incidents"; there was always some Jew who had said or done this or that. You can't fool around with this sort of thing. Capitalism is a precarious system: we're going to be in crisis and war situations, and the temptation to have a scapegoat is going to re-emerge with a vengeance. And who will be the scapegoat in Europe today? Who will it be, if not the so-called Muslims, the people from North Africa, the Africans? It'll be them. It's inevitable;

you can see it coming a mile away. And you'll be partly responsible for it. I'm really sorry for you, because that future is not very far off. Once people's French identity starts being "verified," anything is possible.

AL: *Alain Badiou is making a very serious (to say the least) accusation about you. How would you like to respond to him?*

A. Finkielkraut: The accusation about me is outrageous, but I'm going to try not to get upset. I'll simply say that Alain Badiou and I don't regard the same things as real. We don't have the same idea of reality. Very recently, I clashed with the far right and I was pretty much on my own, because the anti-racist left and the Front National were locked in a strange embrace at the time: I'm referring to the Roman Polanski affair. Fascism operated as it always does, singling out a target for public condemnation and creating a sacrificial victim, who was accused of raping a little girl. And all the politically correct people had no objection to this. Why? Because this man, in their opinion, was a member of the ruling class. And therefore he had to pay. "Those who rail against gang rapes in the *banlieues* shouldn't ask for leniency for the jet-set," wrote Olivier Mongin.[20] He, too, denounced the inequality. He, too, was outraged by the preferential treatment and corruption of the elite. He, too, defended the people (even if it wasn't the same people). Yet the facts mattered little to this champion of the poor. It didn't matter to him that the American

---

[20] Olivier Mongin, "Emballements et déballages (Polanski et Mitterrand)," *Esprit*, 359/11 (2009): 251–4.

justice system's relentless attack on the little "Polack" had nothing to do with his crime and everything to do with his notoriety.

The comparison you make between the Jews and the Muslims could also drive me up the wall, but I'll just say this to you in reply: to my mind, there is the same blindness to the rise of a certain Francophobia as there is to the rise of a new Judeophobia. And it's for the same reasons: the people labeled as "the dominated" are ontologically pure. So if they denounce the Jews but aren't typical French chauvinists it's because they're victims of social deprivation or they support the Palestinians. We're cautioned not to call this anti-Semitism by its real name.

A. Badiou: That has never been the case with me. From the very first pages of *Circonstances 3* I said there was an Arab brand of anti-Semitism, that the greatest attention needed to be paid to it, and that under no circumstances would I have anything whatsoever to do with it. So I don't feel at all implicated. What I'm saying is of a different nature. The European far right has for decades now been based on hostility to Muslims, to what it calls Islamism. You help fuel that hostility by saying that, from the point of view of "civilization," these "Muslims," these Africans, are not exactly like us. They can't be integrated. They hate us. The fact that the Jews were part of "anti-France"[21] was one of the basic arguments of the far right in the 1930s. For the time being, I don't see any fundamental difference between

---

[21] The term "anti-France," coined by Charles Maurras at the time of the Dreyfus Affair, was intended to stigmatize "internal foreigners," or the "four confederate states of Protestants, Jews, Freemasons and foreigners."

the thought processes that are making you so alarmed about the presence of poor, Islamized popular masses in our country and the way the stigmatization of the Jews, who were also poor people exposed to stigmatization (on a massive scale in the Eastern European countries but right here in the garment workshops, too), was manufactured out of whole cloth.

A. Finkielkraut: I think anti-Arab racism is obviously despicable, in the same way as all the other kinds of racism. But the anti-racism of today is like the communism of the past: an irrefutable and endlessly renewable system for explaining the world. It can never be faulted because in everything that resists or contradicts it, it sees a confirmation of its thesis. When Diam's sings:

> My France talks loud
> It lives on dreams.
> It lives in groups, talks about the village back home.
> It hates all rules.
> It cuts classes, most of the time just to fool around.
> Their vocational diploma won't let anyone become a boss,
> so it [my France] gets going and sells dope to the
> bourgeois girls[22]

anti-racist ideology interprets this hymn to noise and slackerdom as a response to pervasive xenophobia. And yet *la France profonde*, which is supposedly racist, praises Rama Yade, Yannick Noah, and Zidane to the

---

[22] Diam's (Mélanie Georgiades) is a rap artist of French and Greek Cypriot origin who had a huge hit in 2007 with her song "Ma France à moi." For the sake of clarity, the lyrics I have translated here are based on the official version of the song, which differs slightly from the version Alain Finkielkraut cites.

skies![23] And unless you simply close your eyes to free public education, quasi-free healthcare, family allowances, rent-controlled public housing, the development of social services, and the architectural rehabilitation of certain neighborhoods in the *banlieue*, the France of Diam's can hardly be said to have been abandoned by the government. We are not living in a racist period of our national history, that's just not true.

A. Badiou: But when the government is a piece of crap, you inevitably end up becoming a Francophobe ... That's only to be expected! The Communards identified with the red flag, not the tricolor flag, which was the one favored by the Versaillais, the people who left 20,000 workers dead. You don't want to use the vocabulary of war, but those people are at war with us. *They're* the enemies, not the workers, who are the main victims of those people. Sarkozy is a lot worse, after all, than a Malian street-sweeper! If anyone is at odds with everything good about this country, it's him, not the street-sweeper. What impoverished thinking it is, tailor-made for the reactionary sensationalist press, to make people believe that Islamism is our number-one enemy! Once again, you're falling into the false opposition between globalized capitalism and Islamism. The real world is nothing at all like that. As far as I'm concerned, Islamism consists of fascist splinter groups; I have no problem with saying that. I have no tolerance at all for such people and I regard them as absolutely dangerous.

---

[23] Rama Yade, a right-wing politician who was born in Senegal, Yannick Noah, a tennis champion whose father was of Cameroonian origin, and Zinedine Zidane, a famous soccer player of Algerian Kabyle Berber descent, are often upheld as exemplars of multicultural France.

A. Finkielkraut: In these times of *indiscriminate* anti-racism, we should reflect on the great lesson Lévi-Strauss taught us: "[D]espite its urgent practical necessity and the high moral goals it has set itself, the struggle against all forms of discrimination is part of the same movement that is carrying humanity toward a global civilization – a civilization that is the destroyer of those old particularisms, which had the honor of creating the aesthetic and spiritual values that make life worthwhile. . . ."[24] I think there is a dimension of universality in French civilization, but there is also a particularism that deserves to be preserved. And, in fact, I agree with Alain Badiou about this: Islamism is far from being the only dissolving force.

---

[24] Claude Lévi-Strauss, *The View from Afar*, trans. Joachim Neugroschel and Phoebe Hoss (New York: Basic Books, 1985), 23.

2

Judaism, Israel, and Universalism

AL: *Alan Badiou, you said you wrote* Circonstances 3 *in 2005 because you were, and I quote, "disconcerted by seeing the word 'Jew' associated by intellectuals with the support that a large part of public opinion lends to policies based on narrow-minded nationalism, or even racism."[1] Alain Finkielkraut, can it be denied that there may indeed have been just such an instrumentalization for the benefit of reactionary policies?*

A. Badiou: I was referring to the absurd chain of reasoning that leads some people to say that anti-Semitism is the secret essence of both hostility to American policies and the desire to break with capitalism. They want to foist on us the ludicrous equation "anti-Americanism = anti-capitalism = anti-Semitism." The question of anti-racism is completely different.

---

[1] Alain Badiou, *Polemics*, trans. Steven Corcoran (London and New York: Verso, 2006), 232–3 (translation modified to conform to Lancelin's slightly different quotation of Badiou here).

A. Finkielkraut: I don't think current French policy is racist. That's what I was saying a little while ago about René Char and Camus. The Resistance model doesn't fit the situation we're in. What's more, all the president's references are taken from the Resistance . . .

AL: *Yet at the same time his close political advisor is the former editor-in-chief of* Minute, *a notorious far-right intellectual, to whom he himself says he owes a large part of his 2007 presidential victory.*[2]

A. Finkielkraut: I'm one of those who were offended by *Circonstances* 3, but at the same time I don't want to accuse Alain Badiou of anti-Semitism because I know what it's like to be the target of an accusation of racism. However, let me read this passage to you: "That the Nazis and their accomplices exterminated millions of people they called 'Jews' does not to my mind lend any new legitimacy to the identity predicate in question . . . Instead, from those limitless massacres, we should draw the conclusion that every declamatory introduction of communitarian predicates in the ideological, political or state field, whether criminalizing or sanctifying, leads to the worst."[3] This radical argument brings to mind, as a counterpoint, a poignant text published in 1945 by Wladimir Rabinovitch, the writer known as Rabi, in the journal *Esprit*:

---

[2] The reference here is to Patrick Buisson, whose strategy of siphoning off some of Front National candidate Jean-Marie Le Pen's voters in the 2007 election through the use of a hard right-wing stance helped hand Sarkozy a decisive victory.

[3] Badiou, *Polemics*, 161.

We have been reintegrated into our status as free men. We have begun to be French citizens again. We have resumed our professional activity, or at least those of us who have been able to. But what we don't speak about is this constant obsession, this secret stabbing pain that lies behind each and every one of our actions or words. No, we will never again be like everyone else. We cannot forget. We will never forget. We were the scum of the earth: everyone was free to do whatever they wanted to us.

The expression "the scum of the earth" comes from Saint Paul: "We have become the scum of the earth, the garbage of the world – right up to this moment" [1 Corinthians 4:13]. But in this case it applies to the Jews and must be taken literally: garbage, that's what they were, from one end of the extermination process to the other. Well, most of the survivors drew the following conclusion from this unprecedented ordeal: "Never again. Never again such rejection, such abandonment, such solitude. Never again will we die like that. Never again will we be swept away like vermin: we will go somewhere on earth where we can recover all our rights as a people." In that "Never again" there was something more than just the redemption of the passive Jew by the heroic Israeli pioneer. The survivors weren't ashamed; they were well aware that it wasn't they who had lost their dignity during the war but the Nazis, their accomplices, their proxies, and all those who were free to do whatever they wanted to the Jews. It's just that they had been the scum of the earth, and Israel, a Jewish state, was necessary so that a situation like that could never happen again in any way. You hear what "Never again" refers to in a completely different way, Alain

Badiou. For you, it's the division between the Same and the Other that is the source of evil. It's the affirmation of identity that leads to exclusion and reaches its climax in extermination. So you advocate a humanity that no inner division would tear apart, and you recognize as legitimate only cosmopolitan states that are "perfectly indistinct in their identitarian configuration."[4] The implicit conclusion is that the Zionists, insofar as they are fulfilling a national destiny, learned nothing from Auschwitz, or are even the perpetuators of Hitler's policies. Such a comparison is an insult to truth and memory. The accusation is even more unfair in that those people in Israel who advocate the emancipation of the Palestinians are Zionist patriots committed to maintaining the Jewish and democratic character of their country.

A. Badiou: I never – let me repeat, never – claim that there is any analogy whatsoever between the destiny of the Jews and Nazi policies. Our problem, as I'm reiterating to you and I will reiterate again, is the policy pursued by the State of Israel and, behind it, the relationship between the people, in their multi-faceted singularity, and a state. Basically, it's clear for you that the extermination of Europe's Jews legitimated the Zionist project after the fact. But the relationship between a horrific massacre and the creation of a state is not at all self-evident, especially if the state in question is located far away from the historical scene where the massacre took place. More broadly speaking, the dialectic you referred to between becoming "the scum of the earth" and the

[4] Ibid., 163.

need to create a nation-state is, in my opinion, debatable in principle and contradicted by the facts.

First of all, in no way has the creation of that state, to date, brought peace or curtailed the existence and expansion of anti-Semitism. There's a Hundred Years' War going on in the Middle East, and the means being used are the dreadful ones that this kind of war, which is neither a civil war nor a foreign one, always uses. And an enormous wave of anti-Semitism has swept over not just the Arab populations but even all the poor countries' populations, for reasons I'll come back to.

Furthermore, I'd like to make a comparison here. It's only a didactic one, of course, comparing phenomena that have completely different intensities. As you know, in the nineteenth century the proletarians – who, as it happens, were organized largely by Jewish intellectuals – also thought they were considered worthless in political society. "The Internationale," their song, proclaimed: "We are nothing . . ." Although there was nothing in the proletarians' destiny that was comparable to the extermination of the European Jews, there was nevertheless no shortage of large-scale massacres, especially in France. For that reason, it was said in the early twentieth century that a "proletarian state" was needed so that that kind of violence and oppression would never be repeated. The "never again" was already being conceived of in terms of a state. People wanted a revolution that would enable a "workers' state" to be built. You don't seem like someone who has a very high opinion of how that idea worked out! So why do you then claim unreservedly that, for the Jews' "never again," the solution must be a Jewish state and nothing but? What's the difference between the two? The extermination of the

Jews is indeed an unspeakable singularity. But, believe me: the "never again" of the Nazi extermination of the Jews as well as the colonial-era genocides, the pogroms in the old Russia as well as the tens of thousands of workers murdered on the streets of Paris in June 1848 or in May 1871, the mass murders in Cambodia, which were based on the difference between "two peoples," as well as those in Rwanda, which were based on the fact that a Tutsi was not a Hutu – all of this means first and foremost that treating anyone as if their existence in our country posed a problem should never, in any situation whatsoever, be tolerated. Between the two world wars there was a very common and commonly accepted reference to the effect that there was a "Jewish problem," including in France. I am outraged that anyone can casually declare today that there is "an immigrant problem" or, indeed, an "Arab problem." We oppose our own identity as a form of stigmatization to people who live in our country and work in our country. "They're not really French": how can you not see that that's always the way the process so well described by Raoul Hilberg[5] begins, i.e., differentiation, identification, segregation, concentration, deportation, and murder? Clearly, nothing about this process should be tolerated, especially not the way it begins. This brings us back full circle to our starting point: any national identification is an identification of the "others," which is an act of differentiation, immediately preparing the ground for legal, or even biological, protocols of identification, which in turn prepare the ground for segregation, which in turn makes

---

[5] Hilberg is the author of the seminal work *The Destruction of the European Jews* (1961).

concentration natural, which in turn . . . If we reject all the successive terms of this march toward extermination we'll be able to force the state to treat equally everyone who inhabits, lives, and works in the country under its responsibility. And it's unreasonable to think that a state, where those who are declared as not belonging here are to be accommodated, can provide a solution and peace, because that "solution," in fact, is merely the state form of segregation.

Having said that, I am not in the least calling into question the historical fact of the Allies' creation of a new state in Palestine after their victory in World War II. It was a convenient way for them to wash their hands of their reluctance to deal with the extermination during the war. The extreme tension that would inevitably lead to the introduction of the identity predicate "Jewish" into the very constitution of that state was immediately apparent. And then we got the Hundred Years' War I mentioned a moment ago and the oppression of the Palestinians that my many Israeli friends all regard as something shameful and scandalous for their own Jewish identity. How do we get out of this predicament now? Well, I just wonder whether maintaining the state's identity attribution isn't more dangerous for the Jews today than creating the bi-national Palestine for which I have been fighting for so long, and which Hannah Arendt had already called for.

AL: *As Alain Finkielkraut reminded us a moment ago, you advocate a unified humanity that would not be torn apart by any communitarian attribution. From your* Saint Paul *book right up to* Circonstances 3 *you make the Jewish people, who have come down to us from* *the Bible, antiquity, and exile, the ancestral site of that injunction of universality, the privileged bearers of that always updatable principle of the rejection of blood and soil. This is a view for which you have been harshly criticized over the past few years by intellectuals such as Jean-Claude Milner and Alain Finkielkraut. For them, making the name "Jew" the very principle of universality is tantamount to encouraging its demise, even if in an intellectually sophisticated way. Could each of you explain your position on this issue?*

A. Finkielkraut: François Furet wrote: "As time goes by, the crime of Auschwitz has not faded. On the contrary, it stands out in ever more sharp relief as the negative accompaniment of the democratic consciousness and the embodiment of evil to which this negation leads."[6] I won't insult you by calling you a garden-variety democrat, Alain Badiou. But, to my mind at least, you're representative of the democratic spirit of the times insofar as, for you, the meaning of the war against Hitler is not, as it was for Raymond Aron in 1942, either "free nations" or "a tyrannical empire";[7] it's either "a single humanity" or "identitarian affirmation." That's why you blame the Zionists for having betrayed their nomadic, cosmopolitan calling by opting for Israel and the regressive path of blood and soil, of rootedness and ethnicism. And let me quote you here: "Israel is the greatest threat weighing upon the name 'Jews.' Today, in accordance with what created its sacred renaissance after

---

[6] Cited in Alain Finkielkraut, "The Religion of Humanity and the Sins of the Jews," *Azure* no. 21 (2005), http://azure.org.il/include/print. php?id=171.

[7] Raymond Aron, *Destins des nationalités* (Paris: Gallimard, 1990), 614.

---

the Second World War, this name can have no meaning unless it is radically extricated from the State of Israel, and unless it is proclaimed that, in its current form, the state is incapable of tolerating, or meriting in any way, the label 'Jew'."[8] A humanity in the grip of identitarian fury turned on the Jews because they were enigmatic and obdurate, and now the Jews, in turn, have succumbed to the demon of identity and are lapsing into particularism. What a shame! What a waste! What a failure! But you're not content with this intolerable indictment; you go even farther. The Jew who puts up a barrier of separation when the time has come to tear down the wall of enmity and hatred between peoples is an old story. That's a very old accusation that goes all the way back to Saint Paul, as you yourself have so remarkably shown, and, unlike so many hyper-democrats who don't know what they're talking about, you're logical, Alain Badiou, and you explicitly reopen the case against Abraham's descendant: the "carnal Jew," proud of his heritage, a fetishist of his genealogy, and deaf to the universal message of the New Covenant. Even as the Church is choosing peaceful dialogue and – despite the deplorable faux pas of the announced beatification of Pope Pius XII – now regards Judaism not as the religion of a past that is over and done with but rather as a living presence down through the ages, aggressive Paulinianism, under your auspices, has migrated over to the radical democracy camp. The

---

[8] Badiou, *Polemics*, 168. The passage in question, from the essay "Israel: Where There Are the Fewest Jews," begins somewhat differently from Finkielkraut's citation of it: "In my view, no greater threat weighs upon the name of Jews today than the politics of conquest, of physical liquidation of Palestinians, of massacring Arab schoolchildren, of dynamiting houses, and of torture, currently pursued by the State of Israel."

most intransigent of theologies has invaded the most atheistic of philosophies! Lévinas says: "The recourse of Hitlerian anti-Semitism to racial myth reminded the Jew of the irremissibility of his being."[9] And you, meditating on Saint Paul and the Holocaust together, call on the Jews to abjure their own racial myth so as to become a universal people. I have no doubt that you'd be the first to defend the Jews against racism, but you nevertheless can't abide Jewish racism, Judaism as racism and even as the matrix of all separatisms, exclusivisms, and racisms. So, to this shocking accusation I would oppose the quiet confession of a perfectly assimilated Jew, Raymond Aron: "If by some miracle I were to appear before my grandfather, who lived in Rambervilliers and who was close to the Ghetto, I would like not to be ashamed before him; I would like to give him the feeling that though no longer Jewish as he was, I have remained in a way faithful."[10] I was born after the war and had no grandparents. But I, too, still want to remain faithful, not to the calling you are foisting upon me but to those for whom and to whom I have to answer: my own relatives. They are watching me and I'm accountable to them. That's what I wanted to say to you; I've been thinking about it for years.

A. Badiou: Ah, families! My "relatives"! The ever-so-decent Camus didn't want to have to choose between

[9] Emmanuel Lévinas, "Being Jewish," trans. Mary Beth Mader, *Continental Philosophy Review* 40/3 (2007): 2008.

[10] Raymond Aron, *Le Spectateur engagé* (Paris: Julliard, 1981), 313–14. Cited in Pierre Birnbaum, *Geography of Hope: Exile, the Enlightenment, Disassimilation*, trans. Charlotte Mandell (Stanford, CA: Stanford University Press, 2008), 194.

his mother and justice, either. But let's not get into that. I'd like to begin by picking up on a word you used that's utterly foreign to my vocabulary. When you say that I accuse the Jews of being "the matrix of all racism," you're using a term that simply doesn't exist in my thinking. The concept of race has nothing to do with any of this. Neither of us considers the Jewish question as a racial question, or so it seems to me. Let's leave that, if it's all right with you, to identitarian, racialist, and biological anti-Semitism, whose archetype is Nazism. I wanted to say that at the outset because I simply do not accept the claim that I make the Jews into some kind of racial matrix or that I accuse them of racism. All that sort of thing is totally meaningless as far as I'm concerned. The problem lies elsewhere. This problem, I also want to point out, cannot be a particular demand addressed to the Jews as such. I, for one, am an internationalist and a communist, in the generic sense of the word. I am therefore, generally speaking, in favor of the withering away of states. What's more, I have spoken far more ill of the French state in my lifetime than I ever have of the State of Israel.

After the last world war, a state was created that originated from a people with whom numerous prominent intellectuals in European history identified. But why did they have good reason to identify with this people, to be proud of their Jewish identity? Because the people in question were non-statist, diasporic, transversal, and therefore, by virtue of their fundamental particularity, destined for and called to universality. Hence the massive presence of Jews in the revolutionary communist movement. It's not for nothing that the Nazi exterminators constantly spoke of "Judeo-Bolshevism." It was this universality, this internationalism, that they wanted to wipe from the face of Europe. Even though I'm familiar with all the compelling reasons that led to the creation of a state defining itself as a "Jewish state," I cannot help but regard it as a spiritual loss for humanity as a whole. You mentioned the word "regression." To the extent that I do in fact think that any strategic progress of humanity must be measured in terms of at least partial de-statization, or of an advance toward what Marx called "free association," I cannot regard the creation of a state with that origin and that destination as representing progress.

Finally, my last comment is that we really have to understand what the issue is regarding Saint Paul himself, since he is at the heart of the dispute. What interested me about Saint Paul, as I expressly wrote, is not the particular content of the "good news," which, for him, boils down to Christ's resurrection. For me, that's just a fable. Consequently, it would be mistaken to think that there's any genuine universality where Saint Paul himself is concerned. Indeed, since the event is fictitious, Christian universality is itself a fictitious universality. As a result, I don't regard Saint Paul as an example of universality; I regard him as an example of a *theory* of universality. Saint Paul was of interest to me as a thinker of what the general conditions of universality might be, not as the founder of Christianity, which I of course don't think can have a universal value, any more than any other religion can. So let me try to sum up in three points the parameters of our debate:

1 For me, the issue of particularity can never be biological in nature. Ultimately, its *raison d'être* lies in traditions and in the state.

2 Jewish particularity, an absolutely positive particularity as far as I'm concerned, comes down to the fact that the Jewish people's relation to the state is historically unique. There is a sort of localization in it for a potential universality, which is basically homogeneous with communism. Indeed, for me, the logic of emancipation requires politics to free itself from the hold of the state, from the terrible fascination with power.

3 Finally, the figure of Saint Paul interests me because of its theoretical implications, not at all as a religious figure. It is the abstract correlation between event, truth, and universality that interests me about Saint Paul, not the preaching per se.

A. Finkielkraut: Real emancipation has not occurred the way you indicate. As Michael Walzer very aptly remarked: "Bring the people into political life and they arrive marching in tribal ranks and orders, carrying with them their own language, historical memories, customs, beliefs, and commitments."[11] The practice of democracy has shown that there is more than just one *demos*, and I'm not sure that democracy can free itself from the nation-state framework without losing most of its essence. Furthermore, nothing was more legitimate for the Jews in the twentieth century, the century of the

---

[11] Michael Walzer, "The New Tribalism: Notes on a Difficult Problem," in *Theorizing Nationalism*, ed. Ronald Beiner (Albany: State University of New York Press, 1998), 206.

Dreyfus Affair, the century of the extermination, than the state option. As for the Israeli–Palestinian conflict, if it is so hard to resolve it's not because the Jews are stubbornly determined to be a nation. It's among other things because, on the Palestinian side, national identity is uncertain. The conflict between Hamas and Fatah isn't just a quarrel between two rival national factions but a dispute over what kind of political association is desirable for the Palestinians. One side says the *ummah*, the other says a nation-state. This hesitation about identity is a very serious problem. The problems also come from Israel and its settlement policy, of course, but it's not true that the conflict will be over the day the Israelis eliminate their national identity. On the contrary, were a majority of the Palestinians to decide clearly in favor of the nation, it would be huge progress. I'm not sure they're headed in that direction, though.

A. Badiou: You're dealing with two totally different issues: the issue of the state in a politics of emancipation, on the one hand, and the issue of the current nature of the Israeli–Palestinian conflict, on the other. The link between the two is not self-evident. As to the first issue, I'd like to point out a contradiction in what you're saying. You begin by saying that the politics of emancipation in the last century did not adopt the international form originally announced. But the fact that they became encased in a national form is precisely one of the obvious reasons for the negative outcome of these attempts. This was something that was known pretty early on, moreover, since Lenin himself, and the Jewish internationalist Trotsky obviously even more so, did not initially support the hypothesis that the revolutionary victory could be stabilized in Russia alone. "Socialism in one country" was essentially a Stalinist invention, wasn't it? If internationalism is an intrinsic given of every politics of emancipation, it's for one very simple reason: the nation-state framework you praise so highly, a historically recent framework, was and still is quite clearly the framework best suited to the development of competitive capitalism. On top of that, it's to blame, even if you seem to regard this as unimportant, for horrific wars. You say that democracy can't do without the nation-state. That remains to be seen. What is certain, however, is that colonialism and war have done quite well with the nation-state, and they continue to do so. There are still, and constantly, wars being fought globally around, on the basis of, and about the existence of the nation-state framework. So I absolutely maintain that no politics of emancipation – that is, politics linked in one way or another to a universal representation of humanity's destiny – can lock itself irreversibly into the segmentation, competition, rivalries, and enormous inequalities created by the nation-state framework today. The socialist experiments of the twentieth century can very legitimately be blamed for becoming tyrannical and dictatorial, in part because they completely took on the legacy of the nation-state framework. Stalinist Russia turned the Communist International into a tool for developing a national state regarded as "the fatherland of socialism" – which is an oxymoron. I think the balance sheet of the twentieth century, all things taken together – the horrific inter-imperialist wars, on the one hand, and the failure of the efforts to create socialism in one country, on the other – should lead us back to Marx's original internationalism, namely that there can be no liberation of all humanity unless we accept the thesis that "the proletariat has no country." So that's my first point.

As for the second point, I would say the following, which may come as a surprise to you. I don't entirely disagree with your analysis of the Israeli–Palestinian conflict. Personally, I am not – to use your language, inherited from Jean-Claude Milner – a progressive, meaning: pro-Palestinian and a disgraceful partisan of the two-state solution, who's not even sure what the basis of that "solution" might be today. I completely agree with you that there's a political and collective weakness on the part of the Palestinians, which is contributing significantly to the deadlock of the situation. I'm sure you understand that a universalist like me also cannot endorse Hamas-type forces. I've always thought that political groups like that, based on a so-called religion, were identitarian groups in the worst sense of the term, typical representatives of closed particularity. They're the symmetrical counterparts of the Israeli far right. These bitter enemies have an identical conception of community in the narrowest, strictest sense of the term and the same shared perspective of a struggle without end. On all these issues, then, there's no disagreement between us. On the other hand, the foundation of a Jewish national home in Palestine can be viewed as something very strange, grounded in religious and historical "reasons" that have no real basis in fact. Clearly, such a foundation would have been inconceivable without the colonial history behind it. But the fact is that this national home, this state, was created. There's no going back on that fact. Unfortunately, I don't think we'll ever see the complete return of the Palestinians to the lands, towns, and villages from which they were so ignominiously expelled. Even the departure of all the settlers from the West Bank strikes me as being a legitimate and understandable but historically unreasonable demand. Anyone who has travelled in that area knows that the settlers are there and are there to stay, one way or another. Since that is the case, I maintain that we ought to turn toward the figure of a bi-national state. This, let me repeat, was Hannah Arendt's position. It's mine as well, and it's the one I obviously think is geared toward peace and progress. As someone who visited the West Bank not long ago, during the terrible period of the war in Gaza no less, I can see no reason why the communities there couldn't live together in their rich diversity and variety. A solution for living together can unquestionably be found. The pool of possible constitutional solutions is well-nigh infinite. Here, as everywhere, anything that furthers the destruction of old nations has my support; anything that breaks down identitarian separations and promotes fruitful coexistence has my support. The more multinational states are, the better they are. If there had been a political leader of genius in Israel who was really determined to offer the Jews of Palestine a new and glorious future, he or she would have asked Arafat to be part of their administration.

AL: *Regarding the Israeli–Palestinian issue, Alain Finkielkraut, we know that you have long advocated the solution of two independent states and certainly not the foundation of a bi-national Palestine. Even apart from the highly problematic nature of implementing the latter, what makes you reject it in principle?*

A. Finkielkraut: The national imperative in conjunc-
tion with the democratic imperative. Hannah Arendt,
whom you mentioned, says somewhere, in *The Human
Condition*, that democracy is the most talkative of all
bodies politic.[12] And, indeed, decisions in a democracy
are based on deliberation . . .

A. Badiou: In appearance only.

A. Finkielkraut: Appearance can become reality only
under certain conditions. You can't deliberate idly, just
throwing ideas up in the air. In order for a civil conversation to take place there has to be a shared language, a
shared historical memory; there have to be basic prem-
ises and a way of living together woven from generation
to generation. Human beings aren't interchangeable,
and borders are not just the sign of a historical fail-
ing that needs to be overcome. They testify – I know
you don't like this concept – to our *finitude*. They also
testify to human diversity. There is Otherness, not
just Sameness. That's why the only just peace between
Palestinians and Israelis requires separation. It should
be compatible, of course, with a Palestinian presence
in Israel, which already exists, and eventually with a
Jewish presence, which seems more problematic to me,
in a free Palestine. But such a separation is the only condition of both real democratic life *and* potential future
reconciliation. Any other solution is false because once
the Arabs were in the majority in Israel the situation of
the Jews would become untenable, since the "one man,

---

[12] Hannah Arendt, *The Human Condition* (Chicago: University of Chicago
Press, 1998), 26.

one vote" principle would then have no basis in reality. And since you mentioned Hannah Arendt, let me quote her too, to broaden the question. We're not here to resolve the Israel–Palestine problem, even if I note with relief that we can tackle the subject without coming to blows. We're managing to talk almost calmly about this very thorny issue. So, in an article Hannah Arendt wrote about Jaspers, there's a passage I think is very beautiful and which I submit for your reflection:

> [J]ust as men and women can be the same, namely human, only by being absolutely different from each other, so the national of every country can enter this world history of humanity only by remaining and clinging stubbornly to what he is. A world citizen, living under the tyranny of world empire, and speaking and thinking in a kind of glorified Esperanto, would be no less a monster than a hermaphrodite.[13]

Technology is promising us all sorts of monsters, all sorts of hybrid creatures, today, but I'm not sure that's the path we should take.

A. Badiou: As far as this issue of Sameness and Otherness is concerned, you know what I think: Otherness is in any case invincible. It has tradition, heritage, the differential disposition of bodies, the disposition of the sexes, and so forth, going for it. One individual is, as such, a huge bundle of differences. It's *Sameness* that is fragile; it's Sameness that is humanity's invention and is practically non-existent. And so to be urgently

---

[13] Hannah Arendt, "Karl Jaspers: Citizen of the World?" in *Men in Dark Times* (New York: Mariner Books, 1970), 89.

concerned about Otherness and defending identities, as though that were a priority, is to reverse completely the order of the problems. Establishing internationalism will obviously be a very lengthy, complex, and delicate process. As for a bi-national state on the territory of Palestine, for the time being I can't see the political way forward, except that a bi-national state is the position of a great many Palestinians, of whom their organizations are hardly representative, and the militant position of a valiant minority of Israelis, who, as is often the case, are the ones carrying the future. My position is by no means to say: "We will assert the greatness and authority of Sameness over the horror of Otherness." Otherness is omnipresent. It's in the order of things. So it's not a question of triumphing over Otherness but of creating a Sameness within which the "living together" that you were talking about is meaningful. And humanity's creative destiny is to expand that possibility, because when it's limited, although it sometimes provides certain internal benefits for the community, it also creates terrible external dangers. Hegel's right about this: communities affirm themselves only through their opposition to and ceaseless competition with one another, and through arduous, tough negotiations. So it seems absolutely clear to me that the perspective that has throughout history afforded humanity the idea of creativity or genuine innovation is consistent with the expansion of Sameness and not with the closure of Otherness, whose objective and inalienable rights are in any case inscribed in the nature of things. That's the first point I wanted to make.

Second, unlike you, I don't believe that the concept of democracy is linked to the closing of the nation. My own experience has been just the opposite. I find it easier to talk with a number of Malian workers today than with many of my fellow citizens, that's for sure. Those who are passionately committed to the necessity of language, tradition, successive generations, territoriality, and borders are undeniably on the far right of the political spectrum. They're not democrats at all. Really, not at all. There is no democracy of identity, for a very simple reason: since the basic make-up of things is Otherness, the discussion has to be about the challenges of overcoming that Otherness. Even between two people that's the way it is! Even in love that's the way it is! The course of love always involves discovering something that, in a way, incorporates difference into something other than itself. To make difference, which is always present, exist beyond itself is the hallmark of what I call thought. Yet the return of identity always implies the defeat of thought, to borrow one of your titles.[14] The defeat of thought always involves its coming up against the insurmountable obstacle of an identity. Affirmative thought, on the other hand, has the capacity to invent and create something that "sublates" (in the Hegelian sense) identity, i.e., something that includes identity in a perspective wider than itself. As a result, a distinction must be made here between the situation and the norms. We know – to use the Israel–Palestine example again – what the situation is. It's that of an extremely authoritarian and militarized Israeli state that deals with problems with the brutality of the conqueror, while, on the other side, there is an extremely divided, dismembered, and largely powerless Palestinian community, which, as it

---

[14] The word *pensée* that Badiou uses here was translated as "mind" rather than "thought" in the title of Finkielkraut's book *La Défaite de la pensée*.

---

is today, is not in fact an effective dialogue partner for a solution to the problem. That's the situation. But I'm not one of those who would turn the situation into a norm. You say: "Take the realities into account." Fine, provided that means going beyond what they are and not repeatedly making them the norm for what is going on. The recourse to tradition is often purely and simply the recourse to repetition. So we ought to have a norm for the situation in the Middle East. Well, when I say "bi-national state," I mean it as a regulative idea vis-à-vis the situation, as another way of viewing it. Similarly, I consider it's always preferable to think that people can live together in a space, whatever it may be, rather than to think that they can't. What we should support and encourage is anything, even in a minimal and embryonic form, that could help them do so.

A. Finkielkraut: It's not true to say they can't. There are Arabs in Israel, while – let's get real – there are no Jews in the Arab countries, and the situation of the Christians there is becoming increasingly precarious. After the Conference of Ratisbonne, violent demonstrations broke out on the West Bank and churches were shot at.

A. Badiou: OK, but let's not forget that Palestinians have also been shot at a lot, and on an infinitely greater scale. I'd like to remind you that the ratio of deaths today is one Israeli for every 100 Palestinians. You have to take that into account . . .

A. Finkielkraut: I completely agree with you, we *should* take that into account. All I'm saying is that, in the definition of "living together," you can't ignore what the Austro-Marxists themselves called the "community of destiny" and the "community of character" ... Mankind has a history but it's not the same one for everyone. We produce the new, but only from what we've received. No one is his or her own creator. Everyone is part of a world that both precedes and exceeds him or her. There is a danger, it's true, that identities might turn inward on themselves. It's essential for political associations to be open and egalitarian. But, by obscuring or criminalizing the dimension of belonging, we neglect, as I said before, the great lesson taught us by Lévi-Strauss, even though he's everywhere acclaimed. The Europeans who proclaimed themselves superior to the rest of the world because of their steam engine and a few other technological achievements on which they prided themselves were taken down a peg or two by the author of *The Savage Mind*, who pricked their guilty colonial conscience and revealed to them the existence and riches of so-called primitive cultures. This French Academician's critique of Western universalism was nevertheless accompanied by a romantic affection for that civilization's particularities. In 1971, at an epoch-making UNESCO conference that caused a furor, he boldly railed against the abuse of language that confuses with racism "the attitude held by individuals or groups that their loyalty to certain values makes them partially or totally insensitive to other values." And he went on to say:

> It is not at all invidious to place one way of life or thought above all others or to feel little drawn to other people or groups whose ways of life, respectable in themselves, are

quite remote from the system to which one is traditionally attached. Such relative incommunicability certainly does not authorize anyone to oppress or destroy the values one has rejected, or their representatives; but within these limitations, it is not at all repugnant. It may even be the price to be paid so that the systems of values of each spiritual family or each community are preserved and find within themselves the resources necessary for their renewal.[15]

I'm not sure if I should completely subscribe to Lévi-Strauss's idea here. I hesitate to abandon the terrain of universality with him and reject the full-face veil or fight noise pollution on behalf of my civilization's values alone. At any rate, I refuse to praise only the zealot of the Other in him or to view as a deplorable xenophobic regression his critique of the global uniformization taking place under the anti-racist banner of generalized multiculturalism. At a time when capitalism, as you yourself say, is moving toward promiscuity and indifferentiation, it's utterly absurd to cast aspersions on that aspect of Lévi-Strauss's thought and a veil of forgetfulness over the dimension of life that he wanted to see preserved.

AL: *But apart from what you're saying about Lévi-Strauss here, apart from his melancholy vision of a world that's finished in every sense of the word – a world in which there's a supply of cultural universes that's not just exhaustible but is really in the process of being exhausted – there's above all Lévi-Strauss's idea that a community of destiny can never be created* ex

---

[15] Claude Lévi-Strauss, *The View from Afar*, trans. Joachim Neugroschel and Phoebe Hoss (New York: Basic Books, 1985), xiv.

nihilo. *There's his idea that a society can never be built from scratch and can never be created on the basis of a system. As he wrote: "Any society is created first and foremost from its past, customs, and usages: an ensemble of irrational factors that are fiercely opposed by theoretical ideas."*[16] *That is, moreover, how he always justified his refusal to adhere to Marxism, which was very unusual at the time.*

A. Badiou: But now both of you are making me say something I don't say at all! You talk about forgetting or completely destroying communities and identities, and about creating something new *ex nihilo*. That's not what I say, nor is it what Saint Paul claims, by the way. Not only does Saint Paul say that there are communities but he also says: when you mingle with the members of any community, be careful to behave like them, to be Greek with the Greeks, Jewish with the Jews, and so on. So nobody here is suggesting that you can make collective groups emerge out of thin air. My propositions, in the hard kernel of my philosophy, actually consist in proposing a solution to the problem of how something new and universal can be possible in conditions of particularity. I find it quite absurd for you to imply that I abstractly contrast a universality emerging out of nothing with particularities that are supposedly separate from it. My first proposition is that there are only particularities. I already wrote as much in *Saint Paul*, moreover. Saint Paul said: "There are neither Jews nor Greeks." But in fact he was also saying: that's *all* there

---

16 Claude Lévi-Strauss, "Ce que je suis," *Le Nouvel Observateur* 74, special issue, November–December 2009: 35.

is. There are nothing but Jews, Greeks, and Romans. He says both things at the same time, and that's what interests me about him, not the disjunction between abstract universality and particular communities. Don't accuse me completely ridiculously of ignoring differences, identities, and communities.

A. Finkielkraut: But, even so, you write that, "from the apostle Paul to Trotsky, including Spinoza, Marx and Freud, Jewish communitarianism has only underpinned creative universalism in so far as there have been new points of rupture with it."[17]

A. Badiou: Yes, absolutely. And any kind of new creation within particularity necessarily includes protocols of rupture with the particularity. If you deny that there can be a point of rupture with a community it's because you assume that it's a closed community.

A. Finkielkraut: No, I'm simply noting that the Jews you praise rejected their own belonging. It's as *not Jews* that they're good Jews. But creative universalism has no need of such a sacrifice, as the works of Hermann Cohen, Rosenzweig, or Lévinas, for example, all attest.

A. Badiou: But, come on, you can't really think that universalism is wholly operative when a religion's particularity is being maintained as an identitarian norm! If that's the case, you better than anyone should understand the way Hamas and Hezbollah conceive of Arab identity and how they make it a transcendent value!

---

[17] Badiou, *Polemics*, 162.

The elements of particularity that are fundamentally resistant to any universalist rupture included, for a very long time, nations, closed communities, the lack of travel and nomadisms, but also, in an utterly essential way, religions. It's clear that, in the tradition of the Enlightenment, contemporary universality (I'm not talking about ancient Greek or Jewish universality) is incompatible with maintaining a simultaneously global and local adherence to the particularity of a religious apparatus. That's why the Jews I mentioned adopted different kinds of rupture with the Jewish tradition in its religious form. They are the modern Jews. But that obviously doesn't prevent any of them from continuing to be identified, to be identifiable, and to identify themselves, as Jews.

A. Finkielkraut: What I see you doing here is bringing back the great Paulinian and theological opposition between the carnal Jew and the spiritual Jew. And I don't want to get involved in that opposition.

A. Badiou: No, I'm not, not at all.

A. Finkielkraut: Yes, you are! For you, there are, on the one hand, the genealogical Jews who stubbornly persist in their religion or identity and, on the other hand, the Jews who turn away from themselves, liberate themselves, and save their honor by repudiating . . .

A. Badiou: That's not a *Jewish* particularity at all! Someone who's a rabid French nationalist is no more predisposed to universalism. And in fact, the majority of those who "saved the honor" of France in 1940, in the face of the Pétainist French state's nationalistic discourse, were internationalists, in particular Jews from Eastern Europe. So would you carp about the distinction between the "carnal French," to whom Pétain incidentally constantly appealed, and the "spiritual French," who liberated themselves, resisted, and saved France's honor? There's no Jewish particularity in this respect. Those who "save honor" are always and everywhere those who place universal norms above immediate national or communitarian belonging. Do you absolutely insist on there being a Jewish exception in this regard?

A. Finkielkraut: No, no. But I would, however, say that De Gaulle was someone very much predisposed to universalism, as was Churchill, and yet both of them were people who were anchored and deeply rooted, who inhabited their history and were imbued with the genius of their countries.

A. Badiou: Insofar as De Gaulle was able to embody a certain French universality in defiance of the Pétainist retreat into identity and collaboration, it was, among other things, mainly because he was prepared to build and implement an alliance with the communists, even in the government itself. That's the truth. That's what made De Gaulle unique, certainly not his nationalism, because, if he hadn't done that, he would have been cut off from the domestic Resistance and he would never have been able to be the figure of liberation he was. He had to break with his own original idea of France ... because, frankly, allying with the communists wasn't part of his *telos*, his singular nature as a military man who had been influenced in part by Maurras.[18]

A. Finkielkraut: And, let's face it, after the sinister episode of the Nazi–Soviet pact, the communists, too, had to adopt an extremely patriotic discourse, attitude, and sentiment, which is reflected in some very beautiful poems by Aragon.

A. Badiou: But what was the aspect of universality in Aragon's patriotic refrain? We know very well what it was: it was communism itself, the Party. Let me quote that line of his again: "My Party has given me back the colors of France." It goes from communism to France, not the other way around.

AL: *Another troublesome subject, as a logical continuation of this discussion . . . Alain Finkielkraut, in 2003, in* "In the Name of the Other: Reflections on the Coming Anti-Semitism,"[19] *you formulated an idea that was controversial, to say the least. The progressive camp, in your opinion, has clearly become the new mainstay of anti-Semitism, particularly because of the "ideology of multiculturalism" that underpins its discourse. Aren't*

---

[18] The "integrally nationalistic" Charles Maurras (1868–1952) was one of the founders of L'Action française and its review, through which he propounded his deeply anti-Semitic, anti-foreigner, proto-fascistic ideas of a state founded on the Church and the monarchy. An enthusiastic supporter of the Vichy Regime (though he later came to distrust Pétain), he opposed De Gaulle, whom he had formerly admired. Arrested in 1944 and sentenced to life imprisonment, he was released to a clinic in 1952 shortly before his death.

[19] In *Azure* no. 18 (2004): 21–33. A version of this essay was originally published in book form as *Au nom de l'Autre: Réflexions sur l'anti-sémitisme qui vient* (Paris: Gallimard, 2003).

you aware that that intellectual framework seems to have become quite convenient over the past few years as a way of automatically discrediting any politics of emancipation that's even the slightest bit radical?

A. Finkielkraut: In "In the Name of the Other" I note that we no longer have the "native-born French [*Français de souche*] and proud of it" blaming the Jews for their irreducible foreignness but the champions of multiculturalism alarmed about Israel's sectarianism. People no longer accuse the Jews of being an unassimilable race or, even worse, an anti-race; rather, like the jurist Monique Chemillier-Gendreau, they say: "Sticking to the idea of a Jewish state means building an apartheid society and accepting in return the construction throughout the world of 'pure' states. Such follies are always in close contact with extermination and sometimes put it into practice."[20] This is not an anti-Semitic critique but an anti-racist one. However, racism has been only a brief and apocalyptic moment in the long history of Judeophobia. And what we're hearing today is a new version of a very old refrain: the Jews are those who resist the preaching of the Gospel, who say no to the New Covenant – that is, to human fraternity. They are no longer blamed for being a race but, once again, as in the patristic teaching on Judaism, for being a chauvinistic, exclusivist, segregationist, and, some even say, racist people. That's really the meaning

---

[20] Monique Chemillier-Gendreau, "Le Retour des Palestiniens en exil et le droit international," in *Le Droit au retour*, ed. Farouk Mardam-Bey and Elias Sanbar (Paris: Sinbad-Actes Sud, 2002), 314–15. Cited by Alain Finkielkraut in "The Religion of Humanity and the Sins of the Jews," *Azure* no. 21 (2005): 28–9.

of the current accusation, and Israel is obviously at the heart of this polemic.

AL: *That accusation has always existed alongside the exact opposite one, actually. The Jews were certainly blamed for that but also for not being integrated anywhere, for being unplaced and unplaceable, for being transversal to any community, as a matter of fact . . .*

A. Finkielkraut: That's right. But the accusation I'm talking about has taken on new vigor with the existence of a Jewish state on biblical land, i.e., on *the scene of the crime*. A very old feeling of disgust vis-à-vis the Old Testament is suddenly resurfacing and taking hold of the most seemingly irreligious minds. This is what Paulinian-leftism is all about. And it's cutting a wide swath. I recently read *La Violence monothéiste*, a scholarly book by Jean Soler, the former cultural advisor to the French embassies in Israel and Iran. The author sees this violence at work even in Nazi ideology: "Hitler was determined to apply the principles he had advocated in *Mein Kampf* to national-socialist politics: no compromises, no half-measures. He wanted to wipe out all the Jews of Europe once and for all, in one fell swoop. It was the logic of all or nothing, the ideology of Jericho."[21]

Things have come full circle: He begins by saying that the victims of Nazism, because of what the Nazis subjected them or their forebears to, allowed themselves to behave like Nazis. And then he discovers that Hitler was actually a disciple of Moses. Soler calls

---

[21] Jean Soler, *La Violence monothéiste* (Paris: Éditions de Fallois, 2009), 386.

this the influence of the biblical model in the West. No sooner did the Jews stop being an accursed race than they became, or became again, racists and even the inventors and propagators of the racist vision of the world. This is depressing, but, let me reassure you, Alain Badiou, it doesn't make me deviate from the line I've been defending for the past thirty years, namely, there must be two states for two peoples, and reconciliation requires disintrication, meaning the dismantling of all the settlements that are not adjacent to the Green Line and can't be part of a land swap. This position has led me to criticize the various Israeli governments and to turn their own criticism of Yasser Arafat against *them*: "He never missed an opportunity to miss an opportunity."

A. Badiou: What comes to mind as I listen to you is that, if the meaning of the word "progressive" is what you say it is, then I have no connection whatsoever with progressivism. First of all, I've never conceived of or made a single accusation against the Jews. That kind of approach is totally foreign to me. To the extent that I've spoken about the Jewish people it was to say that they were a sacred name in our history. I'd like to quote here from that notorious book *Circonstances 3*, on which a coterie of fanatics tried to pin the label of anti-Semitism: "Hence, horrifically affected in its physicality, sometimes, like the Jewish communities of Poland, to the point of having its ancient reality exterminated, the Jewish identity has triumphed through a historical glorification of its name, and through a new strength of belonging and interiority. That this name has a major link to our thought and our history is something that has become clearer to all."²² You don't have to look very far to find this in the book; it's on page 14 [of the French edition]. That is the only thing I've ever said about the Jewish people and I'd like that to be duly noted. I can criticize the policies of the government of Israel, I can think the name "Jew" is being instrumentalized for ideologico-political reasons that are completely unrelated to the Jewish people's destiny, but, as for making accusations against the Jews and saying they're this or that, it's clear that that quickly becomes a way of thinking in which anti-Semitism lurks just below the surface. So, for me, that's not the issue. The issue is what the relationship between universalism and particularity is, for the Jews as for any other collective determination. I know that what generally appears as a dominant particularity in the contemporary world lies in the figure of the state and that the dialectic of universalism and particularity today necessarily revolves around this issue. Since Israel is also a state, it is haunted by this problem, as is the French state. When it comes to this issue, there's no exception. And not only is this incompatible with the fact of saying "the Jews are this or that" but it's even the opposite. For me, Jewish singularity must be treated exactly like any other singularity, namely by taking its history, the history of extermination, of the diaspora, and so on, into account. So nothing you've said has anything to do with me; that's what strikes me.

A. Finkielkraut: It does, actually, a little . . .

A. Badiou: Oh, really? Tell me how.

²² Badiou, *Polemics*, 168.

A. Finkielkraut: Let me go back to *Circonstances 3*. And more precisely to the final essay in it.[23] It wasn't written by you but by Cécile Winter, but you accept it, you introduce it, hence you endorse it as your own. What does it say? That the word "Jew" is the master-signifier of the new Aryans. Translation: Those whose name makes them considered the perpetual victims of an unparalleled genocide are in fact the heirs of the people who perpetrated the genocide. That name, as a result, condemns them to wear not the yellow star but the swastika armband. It's a well-known argument, except that, as a rule, the word "Zionist" is used, not the word "Jew." That word hadn't been attacked so directly for a very long time.

A. Badiou: You're contenting yourself with a reading of Cécile Winter's fine text that ought to make you ashamed of yourself, you who are, often enough, such a good reader in other respects. In the first place, quite obviously, it's not the Jews she says are the "new Aryans"! It's those who claim to represent a superior civilization today, a democratic and consumerist one that has the right and even the duty to impose itself everywhere, including by militarily invading independent countries. Those who regard their utterly particular and questionable system of values, based on the cult of performance and profit, as the "modernity" that everyone ought to respect and emulate. Those who call themselves and who are called "the West." Cécile

---

[23] Cécile Winter, "The Master-Signifier of the New Aryans: What Made the Word 'Jew' into an Arm Brandished Against the Multitude of 'Unpronounceable Names,'" ibid., 217–29.

Winter shows that, unfortunately for all peoples, but first and foremost for the Jewish people, the word "Jew" has become a master-signifier of the extraordinary arrogance of this West, whose core power is the US military. And this is the case for two reasons. One, a reason having to do with *Realpolitik*, is that the State of Israel, which has nuclear weapons, is armed to the teeth, and has won several local wars, has so far behaved (a tragic decision!) as the agent and policeman of that arrogance in the Middle East. That is the only significance of the propaganda refrain *"Israel is the only democratic state in the region,"* because it means: Israel is a "Western" outpost in a strategic region. The other reason is that, via a sort of deadly cult of the Nazi extermination of the European Jews, Western, democratic propaganda, obscenely perched on the piles of dead bodies, seeks to award itself, too, a certificate of essential, unparalleled victimhood and thus to make people overlook the heinous crimes, the unbelievable devastation spread all over, a number of very successful genocides, and an unprecedented heap of national and civil wars – in short, the phenomenal, ongoing violence by means of which the West has consolidated its power and dominance. The word "Jew" in all this is instrumentalized for unspeakable purposes. As the master-signifier of the "civilized" West, it serves as an emotional and historical cover for the most contemporary kinds of imperialist violence. To counter all this, Cécile Winter, I say, proposes a decisive defense of the word "Jew," freed from these state and imperialist operations and restored to its authentic existence, which is that of both the Resistance fighters on the Red Poster and the garment workers, that of both the Bolshevik revolutionaries and the poor

Polish peasants, that of both the universalist intellectuals and the traditional families gathering together for Shabbat. This is why she concludes her essay not by saying anything whatsoever against the Jews but, quite on the contrary, by glorifying them for what they are: an untotalizable set of singularities, a series of proper names. To counter the notoriety surrounding this essay, let me just quote its conclusion. After citing and endorsing this line by Paul Celan in his "Conversation in the Mountains" – "he who had been allowed to live down in the plain where he belongs, he, the Jew, walked and walked"[24] – Cécile Winter states that, against the fatal instrumentalization of the word "Jew" by the new Western Aryans and their imperialist "civilization," one should – let me quote this crucial conclusion –

> take the side of unpronounceable names. Szmul Zygeilbojm, Rudolf Vrba, Robert Wachspress, and Rabbi Benyamin, or Mordechai Anielewicz and Zyvia Lubetkin ... There's no shortage of unpronounceable names; and it would be easy to extend the list, the list of those who have remained by choice with those who are allowed to live down in the plain, and who, by devoting themselves to those who are consigned to the depths, make the light of their name shine for all.[25]

What finer homage can be paid to the Jews, I ask you?

Along the same lines, I notice that those who attacked *Circonstances 3*, whose subtitle is "Uses of the Word 'Jew'," have nothing to do with what I attempted to say

24 Paul Celan, "Conversation in the Mountains," in *Paul Celan: Selections*, ed. Pierre Joris (Berkeley: University of California Press, 2005), 149. Cited in Winter, "The Master-Signifier," 228.
25 Winter, "The Master-Signifier," 229; translation slightly modified.

about that word and are in fact waging a completely different fight, one that involves linking the name "Jew" to the defense of Western "civilization." More to the point, and to approximate Alain Finkielkraut's vocabulary, what they're interested in is building – in fact at the expense of the real Jews, their history, and their extermination – an anti-progressivism, which would function symmetrically with respect to the anti-racism you denounce. A whole bunch of them tried to counter this supposedly hegemonic and secretly anti-Semitic "anti-racism" with an anti-progressivism in which the word "Jew" actually functions as a master-signifier, as an intimidating word authorizing a stigmatization. Who, indeed, would willingly expose him- or herself to being called an anti-Semite? It's the ultimate weapon of the Western "democrats." But I will never give in to such propagandistic blackmail. And I think that you yourself, Alain Finkielkraut, should be wary about this, because this anti-progressivism is a real political figure today, just as progressivism is. And I think that some of the objections you have to progressivism should similarly alert you to the real nature of anti-progressivism and the functions and aims being pursued by it today. The problem, you know, is that, when you start playing around with identities, when you get on board with an identitarian name as a master-signifier, whether it be "Jew," "German," or "French," you can easily find someone more identitarian than yourself.

A. Finkielkraut: I, for one, am not pursuing any aims and I don't think I'm playing around with identities. I don't recognize myself and I don't recognize anyone else, to tell the truth, in those you sometimes allow yourself to call "the pack of propagandists ... who have turned the word 'Auschwitz' and, more generally, the extermination of the European Jews into the 'democratic' stock-in-trade of their propaganda." Despite my family background, I have no stock-in-trade. I'm simply saying that, for a Jew, it's terrible to be called a "dirty Jew," but it's even more terrible to be called an "Aryan" on account of one's solidarity with Israel. That's all. And, in response to that, it's important not to be intimidated, to stick to your guns. For me, it's not a matter of choosing an anti-progressive ideology over the prevailing progressivism; it's a matter of not giving in to this kind of accusation that I do in fact think is outrageous.

A. Badiou: And what do you think about someone being called an anti-Semite?

A. Finkielkraut: That it's intolerable.

A. Badiou: Well, just as you say the progressive camp pushes anti-racism to the point of regarding the Jews as racist, an aberration I have absolutely no part in, you ought to acknowledge that many in the anti-progressive camp now throw accusations of anti-Semitism around extremely carelessly. The best proof of this is that some of those people have already accused *me* of it.

A. Finkielkraut: Along those same lines, let me quote an author you probably don't read but who deserves to be read, and whom I defended, come the hell of progressivism or the high water of political correctness, when he was accused of expressing "criminal opinions": Renaud Camus. He said that anti-Semitism was the "ultimate

linguistic weapon," an insult or an insinuation "which
has only to be uttered for the opponent to be eliminated,
banished from intellectual debate, and literally made to
disappear." The word "anti-Semitism" can't be abandoned because the thing does exist, persist, and show up
even in international institutions. But it should indeed
be used only with the greatest of caution.

A. Badiou: But in that case, I wish you had come to
my assistance, because I was the target of a big smear
campaign like that, too, and I'm afraid you didn't use
your talents to help me because you regard me as a
progressive, hence as indirectly complicit with a suspect
position vis-à-vis, if not the Jews, then at least Judaism.
If I'm saying this, it's obviously not because I want to
turn it into a personal issue; I'm just kind of teasing
you. But I'm saying it all the same because it seems to
me that you have an unacceptable bias. You don't see,
or you refuse to see, that there are distortions of anti-
progressivism today that are very similar to the one you
accuse progressivism of. You don't take into account
facts that are as glaringly obvious as the treatment a
whole sector of anti-progressivism reserves for Muslims,
Arabs, and so on, which has become very widespread
today. I'd be willing to go along with your observation
about the existence of a dubious progressivism if you'd
agree that, in some respects, it corresponds to an anti-
progressivism that's just as suspect. They are in conflict
with each other, and the conflict itself leads to the corruption of minds. So let me propose a kind of treaty
to you. I'm willing to withdraw completely from the
progressive camp as you define it – and if you were still
to find any traces of progressivism in me I'd try to rid

myself of them – but I'd want you to withdraw in the same way from anti-progressivism.

A. Finkielkraut: That prospect of peace is obviously very tempting, like all fantasies. But I'll resist it, because I don't belong to any camp, hopefully, and I don't completely agree with the parallel you're trying to set up. I'd also say, with a touch of irony, that when I myself was the target of an extremely hostile smear campaign, was called a racist, and some people called for my resignation from France Culture and the École Polytechnique, you didn't offer me any support, either. I wasn't expecting you to, of course, but what I've always wanted – and maybe even more so after your own unfortunate experience – is to engage in a discussion with you so as to bring the truth of our dispute to light and so that both sides might overcome their knee-jerk reactions and their intellectual laziness, with all its potentially extreme violence.

A. Badiou: As a matter of fact, I think there's still an element of communitarian knee-jerk reaction in your analysis of progressivism, an element that keeps you from seeing that the norms that should be applied to the Arab countries and the extremist Muslim groups, which I, for my part, regard as fascistic, should also be applicable to the State of Israel or to the far-right groups in Israel. You say that the anti-racists are so anti-racist that they're complacent toward radical Islamism and harbor a kind of ambivalent hostility toward Judaism, or even toward the Jews. Well, I can say the exact same thing to you about the anti-progressives, of whom you're not actually the perfect representative, any more than I am of the other side. In fact, we're having this discussion on the sidelines – we should take advantage of that. What do these dubious anti-progressives do? For one thing, they show boundless tolerance for the State of Israel even though its brutality and militarization are undeniable, and, for another, they use the label "anti-Semite" to discredit anyone who doesn't agree with them. So when you say you can criticize Israel's policies and that you really support the two-state plan – which, by the way, is not the policy of the Israeli government, which in fact supports only its own military rights over the whole of Palestine – it seems to me that you should be able to accept this compromise peace offering without either of us having to deny our own particularities. That's what universalism is all about, after all! That the new truth can unite the particularities that become incorporated within it without destroying them.

A. Finkielkraut: In that sense, I can accept it, but I think it's absolutely necessary and extremely difficult to fulfill both of its requirements: to defend Israel against its enemies *and* to maintain an attitude of critical lucidity vis-à-vis the political deadlock in which Israel, partly through its own fault, is trapped. But neither can I ignore the ideological role ascribed to Israel in the world today, a role sanctioned by some progressives. I mean "ideology" in the sense Hannah Arendt gives the word: the implacable logic of an idea. As long as anti-Semitism is limited to glorification of Aryans and hostility toward Jews, it is a hateful but harmless attitude. It becomes an ideology when it claims to be able to explain present, past, and future history in terms of the machinations of the Jews. And for those who set themselves up as spokespersons for the wretched of the earth, from the Iranian Ahmadinejad to the Venezuelan Hugo Chávez, Israel is exactly what the Jews were for Maurras: a hermeneutical godsend. "Everything seems impossible or terribly difficult without the providential appearance of anti-Semitism," Maurras wrote. "It enables everything to be arranged, smoothed over, and simplified. If one were not an anti-Semite through patriotism, one would become one through a simple sense of opportunity."[26] Now replace "anti-Semitism" with "anti-Zionism" and "patriotism" with "justice for the peoples of the Third World" and you get the two world conferences against racism, racial discrimination, xenophobia and related intolerance organized under the auspices of the UN in Durban in 2001 and Geneva in 2009! Everything became clear and made sense then, and the most oppressive countries were able to offload responsibility for their own shameful acts or their own messes onto the universal culprit. No sooner did they begin to discuss the situation of women, homosexuals, and religious minorities in the Asian, African, or Arab countries than Israel was vilified. It would be naïve to expect such zealous accusers to agree to treat this oh-so-convenient demon as a partner or even an adversary on a human scale anytime soon.

Western societies are less affected, but they're not entirely immune from this way of thinking either. Just think of the civil war in Lebanon, where almost 150,000 people died. It lasted more than ten years, but

---

[26] Charles Maurras, "L'Exode moral," *L'Action française*, March 28, 1911. Cited in Zeev Sternhell, *Neither Right Nor Left: Fascist Ideology in France*, trans. David Maisel (London: Bloomsbury, 1993), 173.

what's the only thing that people in France or Europe remember about it? Sabra and Shatila. That horrible incident overshadowed all the other massacres: the massacres of Christians by Palestinians and the massacres of Palestinians by Christians under the control of the Syrian army. And as regards the killing in Sabra and Shatila[27] itself, people forget, to the sole benefit (so to speak) of Sharon and the Israeli army, the identity of the perpetrators and the name of the instigator. His name was Elie Hobeika and he was a minister in various pro-Syrian governments from 1991 to 1998! He was never denounced by public opinion; he was never investigated by the international criminal courts. Such is the state of collective awareness and memory today. As for our progressives, they took it all in their stride and, aside from a couple of objections, incorporated the Durban anti-racism into their critique of domination.

AL: *You've got to admit that that doesn't amount to a whole lot of people in France. Apart from the self-styled anti-Zionist, anti-racist "Indigènes de la République," who, incidentally, have not really been in the news for a while now, where are the Durban-type progressives in this country? Quite frankly, there's only a tiny group of them . . .*

---

[27] In September, 1982, during the Lebanese Civil War, a massacre of thousands of Palestinian and Lebanese civilians took place at the refugee camps of Sabra and Shatila in Beirut. Israel, whose forces surrounded the camps, enabled right-wing Christian Phalangists to enter the camps and carry out the massacre in retaliation for the assassination of Phalangist president-elect Bashir Gamael. It later became known that the killings were perpetrated under the direct orders of Elie Hobeika, the Lebanese Forces' intelligence chief, as Finkielkraut notes below.

A. Badiou: Yes, you really have no reason to be worried. On the other hand, how about if we put together a file of all the texts by French intellectuals or politicians today who hold radical Islamism to blame for the international situation? You should extend the parallel that far. The anti-progressives have their scapegoat, too. They explain the whole global situation entirely in terms of the clash of civilizations between the West and Islam. I could bring you an enormous stack of statements to that effect every day. So why are you so concerned about a faction that brands Israel as an evil entity and yet you're unconcerned, or even complacent, about an enormous faction that singles out radical Islamism as the cause of all the world's ills?

A. Finkielkraut: Because, even though radical Islamism is certainly not the cause of all the ills, it *is* a real threat.

A. Badiou: Do you honestly think radical Islamism is a global threat?

A. Finkielkraut: Yes, I do.

A. Badiou: You think the Islamist groups are equivalent to the big countries today, to China or the US? Give me a break! They're little fascist splinter groups, nothing more. This gross exaggeration of the "hardcore" radical Islamist threat simply proves that you share the anti-progressives' worldview. You don't want there to be any symmetry. Yet this business about radical Islamism is a fantasy, just as there's a fantasy about the State of Israel. You have to admit that these fantasies are mirror-images of each other. This is proof in and of itself of the ideological polemic raging today. What's more, I can assure you that there are a lot more people in our country who explain everything in terms of the clash of civilizations and the terrible Islamist peril than people who explain everything in terms of Israel's machinations.

A. Finkielkraut: Radical Islamism is doubtless not the world's only problem today, but, given the situation in Iran, Pakistan, and Afghanistan, it's a reality that can't be taken lightly. If the Taliban take over in Pakistan, they'll have the bomb and it will be too late to start worrying then. It'll also be too late when the even more likely day comes when Iran, as is its barely concealed intent, possesses a nuclear weapon. Unless you're wearing ideological blinkers, you can't help but be afraid of this inevitable encounter between ultimate military technology and religious fanaticism.

A. Badiou: I readily acknowledge that the fascistic Islamist groups pose a real problem for states as well as for attempts at emancipatory politics. In actual fact, these groups' power comes mainly from the notable weakness of Marxist-inspired revolutionary politics in the Arab world, a weakness all the Western governments have long fomented, including by financing and arming the Islamists. But it's obviously not this that we're talking about. We're talking about the fact that anti-progressivism regards this threat as *the* major problem. But the history of the world is also being shaped – mainly, in fact – by the present economic crisis, Europe's extraordinary political weakness, and the rise of China.

A. Finkielkraut: I agree with you there.

3
May '68

AL: *Let's turn now to a completely different subject, yet one that's not unrelated to the issue of progressivism. Alain Finkielkraut, your highly critical views on the "spirit of May '68," especially when it infiltrates an institution such as the school, are well known. As it happens, the views of your opposite number, Alain Badiou, on this subject are far from being as enthusiastic as might too easily be supposed. In* The Communist Hypothesis, *for instance, an essay of his that was published shortly after the thirtieth anniversary of the "events of May," we read the following passage: "We are commemorating May 68 because the real outcome and the real hero of 68 is unfettered neo-liberal capitalism. The libertarian ideas of 68, the transformation of the way we live, the individualism and the taste for* jouissance *have become a reality thanks to post-modern capitalism and its garish world of all sorts of consumerism."*[1] *Owing*

---

[1] Alain Badiou, *The Communist Hypothesis*, trans. David Macey and Steve Corcoran (London and New York: Verso, 2010), 44.

*to his hostility to neo-liberal libertarianism, isn't Alain
Badiou ultimately closer to you than might have been
imagined in connection with this thorny "'68" affair?*

A. Finkielkraut: Possibly ... But I'm not going to be
fool enough to try to squeeze '68 into a one-size-fits-all
formula or blame the spirit of '68 for all the problems plaguing French society. What I condemn is the
broadening of the field of struggle to sex, culture, and
school. "I hate servitude as the source of all the ills of
humankind," Rousseau said, and the pan-Rousseauism
of May saw servitude everywhere. The omnipresence
and the omnipotence of the concept of power: that, for
me, is "'68 thought" [*la pensée 68*]. At the time, we (I
played my own small part in this) tarred domination
and authority – or, as Lévinas put it, the master who
conquers and the master who teaches – with the same
brush. We regarded education as a kind of oppression,
teaching as symbolic violence, and so-called legitimate
culture as cultural tyranny elevated to a position of
dominance by the power relations in society. Today, I
would concur with Simon Leys and respond to this by
saying that the demand for equality is a noble aspiration
in its own sphere, social justice, but is pernicious in the
realm of the spirit.

Democracy is the only acceptable political system; yet it
pertains to politics exclusively, and has no application in
any other domain. When applied anywhere else, it is death
– for truth is not democratic, intelligence and talent are not
democratic, nor is beauty, nor love ... A truly democratic
education is an education that equips people intellectually
to defend and promote democracy within the political

world; but in its own field, education must be ruthlessly aristocratic and high-brow . . .[2]

Yet this response has become almost inaudible because protests of the past have taken over the *doxa*. Anti-institutional thinking is triumphant in institutions. The anti-authoritarian slogans we shouted forty years ago now inspire the decision-makers' actions. Look at the schools. What is the enemy of the national education inspectors nowadays? It's the teacher's authority or what they call "frontal pedagogy."[3] The spirit of May '68 has eliminated class ranking, abolished discipline, and done away with podiums. How should this spectacular, belated victory be considered? It's not Marx who can help us understand but Tocqueville. It's not *The Communist Manifesto* but *Democracy in America*. It's not the distinction between formal rights and real rights; it's the discovery of the egalitarian direction our societies have taken.

AL: *Yes, but for that very reason we can see how far beyond the issue of May '68 the issue of the breakdown of authority goes. It is one general trend among others linked to the emergence of mass democratic societies . . .*

A. Finkielkraut: You're right: 1968 wasn't a break, it was an acceleration of the process. The last bastions of hierarchy were swept away, the rules of formality broke

---

[2] Simon Leys, *The Hall of Uselessness* (New York: New York Review Books, 2013), 447.

[3] As Ira Shor defines it in his *Empowering Education* (Chicago: University of Chicago Press, 1992), 96, "frontal pedagogy" is the practice in which the teacher speaks from a position of authority at the front of the classroom to students sitting in rows before him or her.

down, and democracy leveled whatever disparities were still left in our world. The boundaries between adults and children and men and women were dissolved, but so too were those between culture and entertainment, since legitimate culture was now nothing but the dominant culture. And, ever since then, interchangeability has become the name of the game. As a result, two interrelated tasks need to be accomplished. The first of these is to fight for more equality, for the sake of social justice. When you see what happened to the Philips factory workers and employees, who were informed of their plant's closure only the night before the appointed day and were shamelessly offered a job reclassification in Hungary paying only 450 euros a month, there's only one thing you can think: social justice has to be a priority. But there's another task that's absolutely incumbent upon us, one that, as soon as I dare mention it, earns me the label of "reactionary": the task of reining in democracy and restraining the passion for equality as much as possible so as to prevent the world from lapsing into indifferentiation.

A. Badiou: Once again, I'm going to be less critical than might be expected ... and for the following reason. Basically, the point we disagree on is that, in your somewhat elitist, somewhat aristocratic conception of things, the only totally democratic exception you make is for politics. But why should that be so? I can't see any reason why politics as thought, as a norm of collective action, and as an invention, too, inasmuch as it has a history, should be exempt from your general principle that it's impossible for anything of value to be democratic in nature. You mentioned love and art, but you could also mention science and different types of knowledge. Why do you consider politics to be an exception to what can be called "truths," in the sense that what we mean by "truth" is something that's subject neither to the fluctuations of opinion nor to the law of numbers? That's the issue. And I really think your position is self-contradictory, because the ills you perceive are in actual fact, as Tocqueville saw perfectly well, the consequence of democratic ideology's *absolute* dominance – including and above all in the political field. If you accept that something as fundamental as the organization of society, the form of state power, is subject to the law of numbers, how can you expect that everything else won't ultimately end up being subject to it too? If we learn that the law of numbers can determine whether there will be war or peace, what the reaction to the economic meltdown will be, what form of power there will be, and so on, how can you expect education to resist being swept up in the end too? Everyone knows that the gradual dismantling of everything you found so appealing about our schools is due to mass access to education. Democracy – as conceived of in our societies – has ruined education; that much is clear. And so I would tend to agree with you, but I don't think your own views are radical enough! I think you should extend the critique of democracy to its core or hard kernel: political democracy. In that regard, I'm a sterner critic than you are.

A. Finkielkraut: Yes, I do have that impression . . .

A. Badiou: I've never regarded myself as a democrat in the Western sense of the term, any more than any of the real proponents of egalitarian politics has ever been a democrat, moreover, as is well known. And that includes Rousseau, whom you cited. "We shall force them to be free" is the authoritarian heart of Rousseau's thought. The real problem you're highlighting, as I see it, is the intrinsic relationship between equality and democracy. You act as though the essence of egalitarian possibility were political democracy, something that has in no way been proven. You say "social justice," but actually the first automatic consequence of democracy today is enormous *inequalities*, not equalities. Sorry, but that's how it is! So it's not true that there is a special bond between democracy and equality. As a matter of fact, Chateaubriand wrote somewhere that there's a secret collusion between equality and despotism. That strikes me as being truer and confirmed to a greater degree by all the attempts at equality in one world after another. All of this is to say that what I take away from May '68 is absolutely not the libertarian spirit, or generalized democracy, or the abolition of differences, and so on. What I personally take away from it is a political inspiration attempting to be egalitarian in a context other than representative democracy, because representative democracy as we know it, subjected in actual fact to capitalist oligarchy, is both a destroyer of truths and a producer of inequalities. It combines both those defects. So the critique of democracy should be extended to political and representative democracy, and we should ask ourselves what a politics that is respectful of the hierarchy between truth and opinion and yet doesn't produce inequalities might be.

AL: *Alain Finkielkraut, have you ever been tempted to extend your frequent criticism of mass democracy and* *its leveling effect to a questioning of political democracy itself?*

A. Finkielkraut: No, certainly not. And let me quote Tocqueville again: "Feelings and ideas are renewed, the heart expands, and the human spirit develops only through the reciprocal action of human beings on one another."[4] Tocqueville, as everyone knows and constantly repeats, was a liberal thinker. He concurred with Benjamin Constant in defending "that part of human existence which, of necessity, remains individual and independent, and which is by right outside of all social competence."[5] He went even farther, though: "but [the people] could not take part in public affairs at all without broadening their ideas and abandoning set ways of thinking."[6] Tocqueville, in other words, was a republican. He wanted to free people from politics, but he also saw in politics a way to free, disalienate, and relieve them of themselves, of their everyday troubles and their usual distractions. Hence the magnificent tribute that he, the aristocrat, paid to the beginnings of the French Revolution: "I think that no epoch of history has ever witnessed so large a number so passionately devoted to the public good, so honestly forgetful of themselves; so absorbed in the contemplation of the common interest, so resolved to risk everything they cherished in their private lives,

4 Alexis de Tocqueville, *Democracy in America*, trans. Arthur Goldhammer (New York: Library of America, 2004), 598.
5 Benjamin Constant, *The Principles of Politics Applicable to All Governments*, ed. Étienne Hoffman, trans. Dennis O'Keefe (Indianapolis: Liberty Fund, 2003), 31.
6 Tocqueville, *Democracy in America*, 279.

so willing to overcome the small sentiments of their hearts."[7]

With representative democracy, there is always a risk of the citizens abandoning political freedom solely for the sake of their own individual independence or, as Tocqueville already feared, for the small pleasures of consumption. But the contempt that all of direct democracy's advocates display for the non-political part of human life strikes me as ominous. As history has shown, it can lead only to the elimination of that great achievement of modern times, private life.

A. Badiou: But why do you regard today's representative democracy as one of the great achievements of modern times, since you're constantly diagnosing its ills? That's what I find so surprising. How is it that it's precisely in modern, democratized countries, all of which have a representative system of government, that the omnipotence of commodity production and the total fascination it exerts on people has developed so irresistibly? There does indeed appear to be an intrinsic link between unrestrained capitalism and representative democracy. There is every reason to believe that it constitutes an indissoluble unity, cemented, moreover, by the right of free enterprise, which may be part of those private freedoms you speak about. Free enterprise means that, through consolidation and systemic competition, critically important poles of power are created which, as is well known, are

---

[7] Alexis de Tocqueville, *L'Ancien régime et la Révolution française*. Cited in Raymond Aron, *Main Currents in Sociological Thought*, vol. 1, trans. Richard Howard and Helen Weaver (New Brunswick, NJ: Transaction, 1998), 275.

productive and financial ones, poles of power with their own rationale and interests, aimed at summoning every subject to the market as a consumer. To that end, as Marx perfectly saw, these poles of power need to dissolve everything in "the icy waters of egotistical calculation." That's an absolute imperative. And so they also have the crucial function of dissolving institutions, which are regarded as relics of the old world, and ensuring that there exists an atomization of separate individuals with no community other than sharing as much as possible in the delights of the market. There you have it. I think that, for you, that world is a hellish one, but I hate to tell you that that world happens to be the condition and the consequence – *both at once* – of representative democracy. You want to preserve the very thing you think is fundamentally pernicious! I really can't see how you could improve representative democracy in such a way that it wouldn't reinforce what could be called the dictatorship of commodities, the institutional dissolution of everything of value, of everything that's part of a hierarchy based on something other than commodities. You inevitably have to arrive at the idea that politics as we know it, across the whole ideological spectrum, is without a doubt systematically complicit in this dominant vision of people as competitive predators and consumers of things. All the governments rushed to rescue the banks in fall 2009 because the banks were a pillar of their systemic vision.

A. Finkielkraut: They didn't rescue the banks; they rescued people's savings. They prevented a situation like 1929 from happening again . . .

A. Badiou: I'm not saying they didn't! But if avoiding a systemic crisis of capitalism was of such vital importance, it can only mean that we're subject to the unconditional law of this type of organization of production and exchange. Ultimately, all the phenomena you describe – the defeat of thought, the eradication of the hierarchical system of values, the increasing lack of differentiation between culture and entertainment – all these things are consequences of the absolute power of commodities, consequences that were predicted by Marx far more explicitly than they were by Tocqueville, contrary to what you say. Namely, the general dissolution of everything of value, or everything that imposes a hierarchy on thought, in the icy waters of egotistical calculation. This is exactly what's happening today, which moreover proves that, contrary to what has sometimes been said, Marx's prophetic gift was absolutely remarkable, because all this is infinitely truer today than it was in his time. Your objectives could only be achieved by means that are completely different from the ones you're suggesting. You can't, on the one hand, want to preserve the existing political system, linked as it is in a thousand ways to the abominable world of business, and, on the other hand, complain and whine that it has terrible effects on culture, values, and so on. You want to preserve the old world in the new one! And you won't be able to. By your own standards, if the economic and political framework remains the same, things will go from bad to worse. Unavoidably.

A. Finkielkraut: "Every world will be judged," Péguy wrote, "on what it considered negotiable or non-negotiable. All the degradation of the modern world, i.e., all lowering of standards, all debasement of values, comes from the modern world regarding as negotiable the values that the ancient and Christian worlds regarded as non-negotiable. And this universal negotiation is the cause of its universal degradation."[8] But it's not representative democracy that's the issue here; it's the hatred of representation and what can only be called *egalitarian nihilism*: everything is interchangeable, anything can be substituted for anything else because, at bottom, everything is equal to everything else and is equally valid. I would add that the second reason for my breaking with the spirit of May '68 – this occurred to me as I was listening to you – has to do precisely with that slogan that I personally never uttered but was able to hear at the time without being shocked by it: "Run, comrade, the old world is right behind you."

AL: *But it seems to me that the new world Alain Badiou was talking about a moment ago is the world of globalized capitalism. That's hardly a bright future we should be running to catch up with . . .*

A. Finkielkraut: Yes, but Alain Badiou pits a different future against that ominous one and wants to "make a clean slate of the past."[9] I myself believe that the past is our responsibility, that we have to take care of it, and that the old world isn't oppressive but fragile and perishable. So I endorse the agenda Albert Camus set out

---

[8] Charles Péguy, "Note conjointe sur M. Descartes et la philosophie cartésienne," in *Note conjointe* (Paris: Gallimard, 1935). Cited by Alain de Benoit and translated by Greg Johnson, www.4pt.su/en/content/critique-liberal-ideology.

[9] Finkielkraut is alluding here to lyrics from "The Internationale."

in the wonderful speech he gave in Sweden: "Each generation doubtless feels called upon to reform the world. Mine knows that it will not reform it, but its task is perhaps even greater. It consists in preventing the world from destroying itself."[10] Capitalism carries within it the threat of the world's dissolution or contraction, as Adam Smith astutely observed right from the start: "These are the disadvantages of a commercial spirit. The minds of men are contracted and rendered incapable of elevation, education is despised or at least neglected, and heroic spirit is almost utterly extinguished."[11] A society in which capitalism, having become hegemonic, eliminated all the principles that came before or were irrelevant to its functioning would be a truly unbearable society. But – as we've learned the hard way – so would a society organized in such a way that there's no longer any room for private initiative: that's the grain of truth in liberalism.

A. Badiou: In other words, you accept the most fundamental axioms of our society while complaining bitterly about the consequences of those same axioms. I'm really convinced that your position is self-contradictory. And that's in fact why all your statements will become more and more melancholy; they'll translate that contradiction into melancholy. Inevitably, owing to mass democracy's impotence, you'll see everything you value slowly but surely crumble away. The real defenders of what you value, of a society that, by virtue of its very

10 Albert Camus, Nobel Prize acceptance speech, December 10, 1957, www.nobelprize.org/nobel_prizes/literature/laureates/1957/camus-speech.html.
11 Adam Smith, *Lectures on Jurisprudence*, ed. R. L. Meek, D. D. Raphael, and P. G. Stein (Indianapolis: Liberty Fund, 1982), 541.

existence, can keep alive principles other than those of competitive survival, are not and cannot be today's "democrats." The other kind of collective organization, the one that's protective of truths, is not the same as the existing one and will have to emerge from it through a rupture whose contemporary process I can't guess. How can you not see that a politics based exclusively on the law of numbers is obviously homogeneous with a reality based on the market and money? In none of the areas you value would the law of numbers be acceptable, so why would you suddenly find it acceptable for politics? Isn't politics a thought, one of the loftiest and most sophisticated of all? Isn't it a value? Every day, we see what its subjection to the law of numbers leads to. Your beloved Tocqueville, who was already melancholy, had in many respects anticipated this, moreover.

A. Finkielkraut: Sure, but we've also seen what a politics that ignored the sentiment of the majority led to . . . So we have to take the excesses, the atrocities, and the madness of the twentieth century into account.

A. Badiou: Absolutely. But in what way do such excesses and madness detract from the view that everything you cherish is completely corroded by capitalism and its inseparable partner, representative democracy?

A. Finkielkraut: What I cherish isn't corroded by representative democracy but by the egalitarian dynamic that introduces democratic norms into areas where they have no business being, such as the family, education, and culture.

A. Badiou: But wait a second – the egalitarian dynamic isn't the problem! We live in a totally oligarchical society.

A. Finkielkraut: So, to overthrow the oligarchy, you advocate a different type of political organization than representative democracy. And you've said, repeatedly, that the only politics worthy of the name is a politics inspired by the revolt against inequality. But look at how the Internet, for example, works. In light of this new reality, we ought to reread "The Order of Discourse," the fascinating, famous inaugural lecture Michel Foucault gave at the Collège de France. "I am supposing," Foucault wrote, "that in every society the production of discourse is at once controlled, selected, organized and redistributed by a certain number of procedures whose role is to ward off its powers and dangers, to gain mastery over its chance events, to evade its ponderous, formidable materiality."[12] And he goes on to list these procedures of exclusion by implicitly drawing on the example of a utopian society in which they would no longer exist. But such a society exists here and now. On the Internet, in the blogosphere, the order of discourse has been blown to bits. All censorship has been eliminated: equality reigns supreme, spontaneity bursts forth, and speech is unbridled. Intermediaries are bypassed. There's no question of mediation anymore. You have the right to say whatever you want; you can talk about anything at any time; anyone at all

---

[12] Michel Foucault, "The Discourse on Language," in *The Archaeology of Knowledge and The Discourse on Language*, trans. A. M. Sheridan Smith (New York: Vintage, 1972), 216.

can talk about anything at all. The distinction between truth and falsehood has been wiped out; there are no standards anymore, only opinions. Nothing is better than anything else; historical facts and their denial exist side by side, and whatever was left of civility – *the priority of the Other* in human relations – has given way to the heady lure of direct communication between faceless people. With the end of inhibitions, the beheading of authority figures, and the breakdown of decorum, the Internet is '68 preserved in perpetuity. Will that space ever become civilized again? It will require a revolt against democratic imperialism. But that imperialism is grounded in a passion that's too strong for any such scenario to be imaginable.

A. Badiou: You neglected to specify what kind of equality is involved. "Equality" in no way means the generalized equivalence of opinions. That's a really lousy definition of equality. So I come back to my basic elitism, namely, any equality must be relative to the system of truths it refers to. Otherwise, the equality of opinions would be indistinguishable from market equality: it would amount to the interchangeability of opinions, exactly the way money is interchangeable. And, in this regard, we need to return to Plato's largely justified critique of democracy. Society won't be able to function in an acceptable, civil way, to use your term, if it purports to be based only on the interchangeability of opinions. Plato says as much explicitly, and, as everyone knows, I'm a Platonist.

AL: *But not always! For example, in your programmatic text entitled "The Courage of the Present," which was* *published in* Le Monde *on February 13, 2010, you call for a total interchangeability of tasks, and in particular for an end to the "oppressive distinction between intellectual and manual labour."*[13] *For once, that's a vision of the social order that's not very Platonic.*

A. Badiou: The universal Plato is the one who defines thought as the safeguarding of truths. The particular Plato is the one who sympathizes with the Greek conception of the division of labor. I would obviously favor the former over the latter, who, as is clear when you read the text closely, is not very sure of his convictions. The idea that humanity is capable of establishing a community based on the potential versatility of each person's work rather than on a rigid division of tasks does not contradict what I just said about equality. Versatility is clearly a goal for humanity in general to strive for. In particular, it's crucial to eliminate the disastrous separation between manual and intellectual labor, which is the source of class conflicts. Ideally, general versatility would be the necessary norm of any education worthy of the name. But, to get back to the crux of the debate, I think that the egalitarian norm is negated by the infinite substitutability of opinions, because the latter, including in its guise as the Internet, is necessarily controlled by monetary interchangeability. Ultimately, it's very clear that, for the time being, the Internet exists only to the extent that it's structured by great financial powers.

---

[13] Alain Badiou, "The Courage of the Present," trans. Alberto Toscano, http://philosovereign.blogspot.com/2010/02/courage-of-present-badiou-and-communist.html.

A. Finkielkraut: It's always easy to pin the blame on money! But there are passions operating on the Internet . . .

A. Badiou: Yes, but the inscription of those passions, I regret to say, has only been made possible by a computerized capitalism that's one of the most powerful in the world at the present time! All of this is possible only because of behemoths like Google, and so on. And these are products circulating on the Net in accordance with the law of market interchangeability, i.e., the fact that any inscription can be equal to any other one. So I agree with you that we should indeed start with the question of the relationship between the collective body and truths of principle. But the problem is, to formalize this, you can't start with today's representative democracy, since it obviously couldn't care less about principles.

A. Finkielkraut: I don't think capitalism is stirring up the passions unleashed on the Web. Instead, I think there's a disturbing homology between the law of interchangeability and the assertion that all practices, behaviors, and styles are equal. And, as I was listening to you, I thought of that line of Flaubert's that Barthes analyzed in the pages of *Le Nouvel Observateur* in 1978: "I write not for today's reader, but for every reader who might appear, as long as the language lasts."[14] What concerned Barthes and gave him food for thought was the fact that Flaubert didn't link literature to doctrines

---

[14] Roland Barthes, "Day by Day with Roland Barthes," trans. Richard Howard, in *On Signs*, ed. Marshall Blonsky (Baltimore: Johns Hopkins University Press, 1985), 109. The line occurs in a letter Flaubert wrote to George Sand on December 4, 1872.

or to revolutions in mentality but to a *form*: the French language. And Barthes didn't see that form as being something that would last forever. The French language might well die. And tomorrow the French might speak a post-national language, i.e., a language totally independent of literature, traditional syntax, and the rules of correct usage. We are closer to that tomorrow now than Barthes was when he expressed his concern, because the very idea of correct usage has disappeared from education – and it's not the MEDEF [employers' federation] that has put that disappearance on the syllabus but progressive pedagogy. What Barthes foresaw has come to pass: "In other words, it's *today* that we need to be thinking of Classical Writing as released from the *Durable* in which it was embalmed. Now that it's no longer caught in the Durable, it becomes *New*."[15] And the same Barthes who, in *Mythologies*, had ridiculed all the symbols of "*francité*" [Frenchness] asserted in his final seminar, *The Preparation of the Novel*, that the work that needs to be written should be *filial*. That's where he stood. And that is, *mutatis mutandis*, where I stand, too.

A. Badiou: Once again, let me try to list the points we agree on. We agree on the fact that a certain May '68 was actually only an acceleration or a consolidation of strong trends toward the general substitutability of opinions, objects, and bodies. This May '68 basically contributed to the dissolution of everything in the icy

---

[15] Roland Barthes, *The Preparation of the Novel: Lecture Courses and Seminars at the Collège de France (1978–79 and 1979–80)*, trans. Kate Briggs (New York: Columbia University Press, 2010), 295.

---

waters of capitalism. And so we agree on the fact that the solution doesn't lie in that direction, in the promotion of that sort of substitutability. Furthermore, we agree that, in reality, the consideration of what the community is really capable of, or its civil humanization, or its maximal existence, is clearly linked to the preservation of a certain number of principles. This means that we're both opposed to a certain strain of libertarianism still lurking in the situation today, and we also agree that not everything is interchangeable and that there are hierarchies in the order of thought. These are, after all, two boundaries within which we're placing our discussion, but I can clearly see that you're trying to pin the main blame for this state of affairs, which you think is disastrous, and one of whose black marks is the demise of language, something I couldn't agree more about – you're trying to pin the main blame for all of this on progressivism's passion for equality. That's the issue on which I disagree totally with you. The root cause of this situation is obviously a world in which nothing has any value or power except what can circulate in a form that must always be able to be measured in monetary terms. And that's something Marx foresaw: the old hierarchies, institutions, and values would gradually be eliminated in the universal circulation controlled by capitalism. I wonder why, as is patently obvious, you're trying to find excuses for capitalism. It's clear that you don't want to go so far as to condemn it, and I just can't understand why not. After all, you don't need to embrace the legacy of the communist experiments of the twentieth century for that! Even before deciding what assessment should be made of state communism, it's still possible to take a stand on the fact that all the vices you denounce in the development of French society today can be blamed largely on capitalism, which also means that they can be blamed on the successive governments that were responsible for managing society. Everything you're complaining about is contemporaneous, after all, with the demise of a powerful, tough, and well-structured opposition to the dominant oligarchy. Logically, you ought to be nostalgic for the time when there was a powerful Communist Party in France – that should be your biggest regret! The Communist Party was one of the most effective conservative defenders of everything you love. It was one of the defenders of education, of the hierarchy of labor, and of the nation. It was the Communist Party that said: "Let's produce French" [*Produisons français*]; it was the Party that kept things under control in the *banlieues* and in the factories. It's not surprising that it was one of May '68's targets. There was something that connected the French Communist Party to everything you love, which I, for one, would call – because I love it, too – *French charm*, meaning a paradoxical combination of love of novelty and passion for order and rules. A French charm reflected in our language, in its classicism, in its transmission in school via the *dictée*, that spelling test that's still a mass exercise and is even broadcast on TV. This charm is constantly being attacked and destroyed by the outright unleashing of contemporary globalized capitalism's energies in this country.

AL: *Actually, the lack of any dimension of critique of capitalism in your thinking is surprising, Alain Finkielkraut. One might even get the impression that that aspect of things simply doesn't interest you and that*

*you've decided to exclude it from your field of vision.
Yet there are some notable examples of thinkers in the
twentieth century – I'm thinking of Walter Benjamin,
in particular – whose radical rejection of the ideology
of progress existed side by side with an equally strong
critique of commodity fetishism . . .*

A. Finkielkraut: You'd have to be blind or ignorant not
to see that capitalism, especially in its current version
– finance, shareholder, post-entrepreneurial – increases
inequalities and causes real human tragedies. I'm also
convinced of the need to fight our society's tendency
not to make any room for excellence or honor and to
be wholly controlled by the profit motive. But a social
critique denouncing the spirit of capitalism and at the
same time endorsing the democratic scorn of any kind of
greatness or distinction is, under its trenchant exterior,
a very inadequate and ultimately tame social critique.

A. Badiou: And yet that's precisely what the initial critique of capitalism was! It's striking that what we are
indeed seeing today is the breakdown of all traditional
forms of authority, and for what I think is a very simple
reason: the hierarchy of opinions, not their equivalence,
creates a subjectivity that's at odds with capitalism.
Capitalism requires a separate, individual, consumerist
subjectivity. And even the Internet is a tool for molding
a subjectivity of that type, a solitary subjectivity that
considers its most off-the-cuff opinion worthy of being
communicated to the whole world, equal to all the
others. But what is this, actually? It's capitalism's dream
subject! Capitalism certainly doesn't want a subject who
thinks there are values that are non-interchangeable.

What could it do with a subject who loves beauty, love, revolutionary politics, or pure mathematics, or even with subjects like you and me who love their country? It wants nothing to do with them, because subjects like that are completely incompatible with the kind of circulation it organizes.

A. Finkielkraut: That "it" bothers me a bit, though – it becomes a subject in its own right . . .

A. Badiou: But it's just a metaphor for the system. Let's call it "K" if you prefer, *das Kapital*.

A. Finkielkraut: That bothers me even more!

A. Badiou: It's only normal that such a powerful social organization, and one that has moreover spread all over the world, would mold its own type of subjectivity. So my question to you is: You'd like for there to be other kinds of subjectivities, different kinds, but where are you going to get them from if you begin by approving of the means of production of the very subjectivities you're opposed to? Capitalism destroys everything it has no need of.

A. Finkielkraut: Look, maybe there's a biographical fact I should mention here. I'm not the son of a big capitalist, but I do come from a family of businessmen. When my paternal grandfather, Aaron Finkielkraut, arrived here from Poland in the late 1920s, he opened a fine leather goods business with his two sons, on rue Jean-Pierre Timbaud in Paris. The business was quite successful. So my father was actively involved in the system that I, like everyone around me, hated in the 1970s. One day, though, I wondered if I should really be ashamed of him. Would he have been morally superior if he'd been a teacher, a researcher, or a civil servant? That simple question roused me from my dogmatic slumber, and I took my distance from a way of thinking that involved such an unfair rejection. I can no longer go along, as you still do, with a program that sets capitalism up as a principle of evil. There are, of course, other reasons as well behind this break. Do you believe all social violence can be attributed to capitalist exploitation? When we hear that some young men wearing balaclavas entered a public school gym and beat up a student who was taking a hip-hop class, we're flabbergasted and anxiously wonder how we could have gotten to this point – to this explosion of barbarism and this out-and-out surrender to what is pompously called "the culture of the *banlieues*." The answer to these questions cannot be found in *The Communist Manifesto*.

A. Badiou: Oh, come on, you're obviously caricaturing things . . . You have to decide on what level of generality you want us to be talking. You're suddenly descending to the level of a single anecdote! I asked you why you were making excuses for capitalism's responsibility whereas you aren't making any at all for the progressive camp, and you answer with an anecdote about a fight in a hip-hop class . . . But now, if you'd like, we can in fact go down to the level of concrete situations. The gradual erosion of the boundaries between adult and adolescent, and between adolescent and child, is one of the major factors contributing to the situation you describe. But you can't get around the fact that this erosion itself is

due largely to the fact that adolescence is a vital consumer target for contemporary capitalism.

A. Finkielkraut: That's absolutely true.

A. Badiou: People want sneakers, cell phones, and so on.
So they couldn't care less about school, since it has no
direct connection with this virulent consumerism! Those
are the facts of the matter. It's consequently very easy to
describe these concrete situations phenomenologically.
We can indeed go right from the generality of capital
to the dramatic situations you mentioned, which are
part of the breakdown of institutions and hierarchies,
in particular of the breakdown of the teacher–student
relationship – a relationship that's unfathomable to
those who can dream only of instant gratification. That
kind of hierarchy makes no sense to them anymore,
quite simply because the teacher is a loser – he or she
doesn't even have the right shoes! When you're at that
point ... But they've been *allowed* to think as much.
The overall system has even *encouraged* them to think
that way.

A. Finkielkraut: Good point. I couldn't agree more.

A. Badiou: Let's go back for a moment to what you
were saying about your father. Unlike your parents,
mine were civil servants. But, as I explained a little while
ago and will now repeat, I, for my part, advocate the
withering away of the state. I'm in favor of a society
that would be organized on the basis of free association,
maybe a thousand or a couple of thousand years from
now, because it would be an educated society, in Plato's

sense of the term – a society in which everyone's a philosopher! At any rate, it would be a society in which the functions of the state, as a separate power, would be distributed over the entire surface of society. Does this mean I'm going to say I'm ashamed of my father, who was the epitome of the man imbued with the ideology of government service? He was the mayor of Toulouse, he was a *député*, etc. Well, I'd come to the same conclusion as you and say no, because, as long as there's a state, it's better off having good public servants than crooks. And, as long as there's capitalism, we're better off with an honest small businessman than with a billionaire mafioso.

A. Finkielkraut: It's that "as long as" that divides us.

A. Badiou: Maybe, but I don't see why you need to validate the system as a whole.

A. Finkielkraut: No doubt, but for me it still entails the need to validate the concept of the state *and* the spirit of enterprise. Both of them.

A. Badiou: You're redeeming both of our fathers! That's great.

4

Communism
(Past and Future)

AL: *The sons reconciled with their fathers: that's a bold conclusion, but it's ultimately consistent with your critique of a certain spirit of '68. Still, there's something that inspires real affection for May '68 in you, Alain Badiou. It was basically the last time in French history, at least up until now, that the red flag flew over the entire country, in factories and working-class neighborhoods. As a matter of fact, I wanted to continue this conversation by asking Alain Finkielkraut how he views the current resurgence of the "communist Idea" and the partial return to favor of political radicalism that's reflected in the growing audiences of Alain Badiou and a few other people today. How do you interpret this period of "détente," which has come after the absolute dominance of anti-Marxism in media and intellectual circles?*

A. Finkielkraut: I think there's something paradoxical about the way some materialist thinkers want to shield the communist Idea from, or set it above, its actual achievements. To me, the Idea seems irredeem-ably compromised by all the forms of real communism that have ever existed. The communist reality that we've known, and which isn't completely gone yet, has betrayed communism – not in the sense that it has per-verted it but in the sense that it has exposed it for what it really is. And to get something straight right away, it's when everything is political that everything is bound to become like a police state. The great contribution of modern times to civilization was *the art of separation*: the separation of Church and state, the separation of civil society and the political community, the separation of public and private life. "Our homes, our castles." Communism condemns this compartmentalization (the rights of man, Marx said, are the rights of the egotistical man, separated from the community and public affairs) and then, when it has the means to do so, destroys it. It nationalizes people's innermost feelings, it requisitions their private thoughts and invades all the sanctuar-ies of personal dignity. This takes place in two stages: the stage of the ideal and the stage of terror. I recently read an extraordinary book entitled *The Whisperers*, by Orlando Figes, a great historian of the Russian Revolution.[1] Why "the whisperers"? Because, as Isaac Babel wrote during the Stalinist era, "Today a man only talks freely with his wife – at night, with the blankets pulled over his head." Yet Figes' investigation begins in 1917; that's what's so interesting. To understand the violence and the fear, he goes back to the initial efferves-cence. The revolution has just broken out; the scene is

---

[1] Orlando Figes, *The Whisperers: Private Life in Stalin's Russia* (London: Picador, 2008).

the Smolny Institute, Bolshevik headquarters. Elisaveta Drabkina hasn't seen her father for twelve years. In 1905 he had gone into hiding. She has forgotten what he looks like and only knows his Party pseudonym, "Sergei Gusev." Suddenly, just as she's finishing her meal, a small but muscular, handsome man in military dress and a pince-nez, trailed by a retinue of Party workers, enters the smoke-filled dining hall. The newcomer sits down at the long central table and eats his soup with a spoon in one hand while signing papers that are placed before him with the other. Elisaveta Drabkina then hears someone call him "Comrade Gusev." Still hungry, she approaches him and says simply: "Comrade Gusev, I am your daughter. Give me three rubles for a meal." "Of course, comrade," he replies. And without further ado her father hands her a three-ruble note. Lenin loved this story. He saw in it the Bolshevik ideal of total dedication to the revolutionary cause. He loved the new, *unseparated* man who would never allow himself to be distracted by his personal ties from history in the making and from the love of humanity. The implementation of a permanent, all-embracing, omnipresent panoptical force monitoring everyone's life and everything about it is not the denial but rather the *result* of that original revolutionary enthusiasm. "The so-called sphere of private life cannot slip away from us, because it is precisely here that the final goal of the Revolution is to be reached," wrote Anatoly Lunacharsky three years after Lenin's death.[2]

At first, there were constructivist architects who sought to break down the wall of intimacy by building

---

[2] Cited in Figes, *The Whisperers*, 8.

"communal houses" in which the inhabitants shared all possessions, including clothing and underwear, among themselves, domestic chores were assigned to various teams on a rolling basis, and everyone slept in an enormous dormitory, separated by gender, with private rooms available for sex. Later, there were community apartments. Promiscuity and control are the natural offspring of utopia. In a nutshell, the basic ontological decision of modern times consists in building and defending a world where *nothing is everything.* Communism challenges that decision and thus carries the totalitarian catastrophe within it the way storm clouds carry the storm. "There is history, and there is something else, simple happiness, the passion of human beings, and natural beauty," wrote Camus.[3] The communist Idea cannot be exonerated of the crimes of communism, because it is the negation of that "something else."

AL: *I'm not sure that's the best anti-communist anecdote you could have come up with. It can be found almost word for word in the New Testament: "Who are my mother and my brothers? Whoever does the will of God is my brother and sister and mother," Christ says in the Gospel according to Mark, for example. This imperative of breaking free from the bonds of kinship in order to join a spiritual community isn't a Stalinist invention; it has glorious antecedents.*

---

[3] Albert Camus, "Réponse à Emmanuel d'Astier de la Vigerie," *Essais*, vol. 2 (Paris: Gallimard, 1965), 368. Cited in Marcel J. Mélançon, *Albert Camus: An Analysis of his Thought*, trans. Robert Dole, http://classiques. uqac.ca.

A. Finkielkraut: On the contrary, I think the anecdote is very instructive. It's when there's nothing that is not shared by everyone that everything ends up being taken away; it's when there's nothing that is not political that everything ends up being turned over to the government's inquisition. My conclusion is that the communist hypothesis is not the right one.

A. Badiou: My own comment is that, when the word "communism" made its first appearance in the nineteenth century, specifically around 1849, it represented a historical hypothesis of such magnitude that, as far as Marx was concerned, everything that came before was like prehistory. Communism is in a way the name, or the beginning, of another historical age in humanity's existence. So to make this idea – that another generic sequence of humanity is going to begin – stand trial before the court of seventy years of dictatorship in Russia, so as to do away with it for once and for all, is absurd. "Democracy," or any other great historico-political category, could be tried in the exact same way. The communist experiments of the twentieth century should be treated as attempts to resolve the first problem the nineteenth century passed down to us, namely, is it really possible to seize power? Creating an efficient special civil war board was the Party's doctrine. Next came a state experiment that was very paradoxical, since, as is common knowledge, the desire to have done with the figure of a separate state is inherent in the communist Idea. Furthermore, the political totalitarianism you mentioned – the elimination of the distinction between private and public life for the sake of the primacy of politics – is a very paradoxical idea, too, since

Marx clearly explained that, inasmuch as politics is the organization of class struggle, communism is the end of politics.

Ultimately, what appeared as communism in the twentieth century involved particular lessons about the issues of organization, insurrection, and popular war, hence concepts that are all related to the category of power. But that category refers precisely to what must wither away under communism. It was therefore a limited historical experiment and, in a sense, a paradoxical one, as compared with the essence of what is meant by the word "communism." The only incontestable success of these experiments was the initial military victory, the seizure of power, and so, with regard to these brief dictatorial experiments, one can speak of a primitive communism, or even, to use one of Lenin's terms, a "war communism." It follows from these obvious facts that I agree in a way with everything you're saying, except that it would be like saying that the Spanish Inquisition was the perfect epitome of two thousand years of the Christian Idea's existence. When it comes to the word "communism," we need to go back to its true meaning, its generic meaning, namely, the hypothesis that human societies do not need to be governed by the principle of private interest. This doesn't mean that the individual is absorbed into the community or any such thing. It simply means that it's possible not to be totally controlled by profit-driven oligarchical poles of power of which the entire political system is actually the lackey. If "communism" denotes a society in search of an immanent principle different from private interest, then we should regard the past century's seventy years of communist experimentation as what they really were, namely, a tiny differential beginning – and, like all beginnings, still rocky – of a historical sequence that will probably extend over several centuries. I'd add that the fact that societies have been under the domination of the rich and powerful has, for its part, been the case for thousands of years. So seventy years of communist experimentation are put in the dock and are told: "Well, you failed to resolve the problem passed down from thousands of years of natural domination, so your signifier has lost its credibility!" I, for one, find this to be a poorly conducted, really poorly run trial. A word, "communism," is tried by a court of history that no other one would ever be tried by. In particular, the connection between communism and totality is a connection that one can attempt to argue with regard to the organization of countries in which a party-state dominates, but the historical form of the party-state has no natural or essential relationship with communism. There's absolutely no reason why communism should be the reign of totality. It's a lot more likely that communism would be the reign of multiplicity. I feel all the less implicated by this to the extent that, if you take any one of my books, you'll see that it presents itself as a critique of the One and totality. The first theorem of *Logics of Worlds*[4] is "The All does not exist." And the central thesis of *Being and Event*[5] is that the form of being is the multiple-without-one.

So, in the first place, I have nothing to do with any "totalitarianism" whatsoever and, in the second place,

---

[4] Alain Badiou, *Logics of Worlds*, trans. Alberto Toscano (London and New York: Continuum, 2009).

[5] Alain Badiou, *Being and Event*, trans. Oliver Feltham (London and New York: Continuum, 2005).

---

the word "totalitarianism" merely denotes an interpretive figure, not of communism in general but of the experiment associated with a few decades during which the Bolsheviks and, later, the parties affiliated with the Third International seized power. It is philosophically incorrect to subsume "communism" under "totalitarianism." And it is, moreover, dangerous to do so when the basic question today has become: How can we bring about a society capable of protecting the principle of the coexistence of multiplicities from unrestrained free-market savagery? To approach this question from a clarified and constituted perspective, I think we absolutely need the word "communism." It is "communism" that has denoted and will continue to denote the strategic alternative to what you yourself complain about.

A. Finkielkraut: But a hypothesis positing that the prehistory of human society has come to an end with capitalism is a chilling thought, because it calls for the destruction of the old world and its representatives. Your grand alternative is too absolute not to be ruthless. While waiting for politics to be abolished, communism conceives of and practices it as a total war between the future and the past, history and prehistory, humanity and its enemies. Well, no! As Hans Jonas says in *The Imperative of Responsibility*, authentic man with his greatness and wretchedness has always existed. Even in the future, every contentment will breed its discontent, and "we shall have to resign ourselves to the fact that we must learn from the past what man is, that is, what he is capable of being, both positively and negatively, and this lesson provides all we could wish for to make us thrill or tremble, hope and fear, as well as criteria for evaluation, hence criteria for a demand we address to ourselves."[6] And, as Solzhenitsyn says in *The Gulag Archipelago*, the line dividing good and evil separates neither states nor classes nor parties; it cuts through the heart of every human being, and "who is willing to destroy a piece of his own heart?"[7]

The twentieth century, which was a century of massive antinomies and staggering alternatives, compels a thinking of entwinement, not, of course, to abandon or tone down the demand for social justice but to respond to the hubris of communism.

A. Badiou: Once again, I feel as if what you're saying has nothing at all to do with me, for one simple reason: despite Marx's "revolutionary" metaphor, according to which the history of humanity as class struggle is merely the prehistory of communism, there's absolutely no reason to think that there's a binary opposition between history and prehistory. A little while ago you identified with the thinking of the Moderns. Well, that thinking appeared at a given moment in time and spread naturally, so why do you assume that there was a sort of complete break between it and the ancient world? Clearly, nothing separates prehistory from history in a concrete situation. That's an absurd way of thinking. What can be called "communism" is an enormously long process with gradually differentiated stages. This

---

6   Hans Jonas, *Le Principe responsabilité: une éthique pour la civilisation technologique*, trans. Jean Greisch (Paris: Flammarion, 1999), 413 (my translation; the sentence does not appear to be in the English edition of the book).
7   Aleksandr Solzhenitsyn, *The Gulag Archipelago: 1918–1956*, vol. 3, trans. Thomas P. Whitney (New York: Harper & Row, 1978), 168.

process involves the emergence, right from within the situation as it is, of fragmentary, successive, etc., points of support for something that deserves a different name. What we're dealing with is a vision of immanent historical origin, which, even if it involves moments of rupture or events of creation, nevertheless does not appear as a binary choice or as something surging up *ex nihilo*. Again, you're making an amplifying induction, as the epistemologists say: you're tacking onto the generic dimension of communism some very particular aspects of the experimentation that took place in the twentieth century, whereas the whole task today is to assess the latter in such a way that it won't be repeated. Which is exactly the way it happens with any historical process: there are always course corrections. For example, it's well known that democracy in Greece began as if it were perfectly compatible with slavery, the exclusion of foreign aliens, the lack of any political presence of women, and constant, extremely savage colonial wars. For a long time and in many places, a more inclusive democracy was nevertheless still censitary: you had to be in possession of a certain fortune to vote. Women didn't get the vote in France until 1945 – in other words, only yesterday. There were fierce struggles over all these issues, and it even required uprisings for suffrage to become really universal. It will be the very same thing with communism, which will gradually reduce all the "big differences" in terms of social organization: differences between the city and the country, rich and poor, manual and intellectual labor, women and men ... A course correction of systems that were originally put in place under the name of "communism" will occur in stages, via fierce confrontations. To reject such a perspective, while considering it a perfectly natural one for democracy, can only mean that one is resigning oneself forever to the superiority of the rich and the inferiority of workers, farmers, and low-level employees.

A. Finkielkraut: Would you accept the intertwining of good and evil? Would you say that authentic man has always existed, with his bliss and torment, his justice and his guilt, or, as Hans Jonas, once more, puts it: "in short – in all the *ambiguity* that is inseparable from his humanity?"[8] These, it seems to me, are questions that the history of the communist Idea allows us to ask.

A. Badiou: I can't see why the history of the communist Idea would allow us to return to a metaphysics of good and evil as simplistic as the one you're suggesting.

A. Finkielkraut: Because, with slogans such as "Man is the future of man" or "To change man at the deepest level," communism is a lot more simplistic than what I'm trying to say . . .

A. Badiou: But I don't see why it would be *that* metaphysics that would return . . . The human heart is divided between good and evil – big deal!

A. Finkielkraut: The problem is that this was completely forgotten. The problem is that a simplistic anthropology tried to inscribe itself into history. "I write *nihil*

---

8 Hans Jonas, *The Imperative of Responsibility: In Search of an Ethics for the Technological Age*, trans. Hans Jonas and David Herr (Chicago: University of Chicago Press, 1984), 200.

on anything that has been done before," Mayakovsky coolly declared, and you, to justify your refusal to allow the communist Idea to be judged by a historical epoch that lasted seventy years, you say that domination, subjugation, and man's exploitation of man have existed throughout human history. And you have even gone so far as to write: "Whoever does not illuminate the coming-to-be of humanity with the communist hypothesis . . . reduces humanity, as far as its collective becoming is concerned, to animality."[9] So you do in fact pit great abjection or irremediable mediocrity against future communism. That kind of dualism promotes crime, because it's not just the past that it repudiates and condemns to death but inevitably the people who embody that past as well.

A. Badiou: No way! Why do you assume that a past is repudiated by its future? It's as if you were to say that, ultimately, the scientists who established Galilean physics, which grew out of a critique of Aristotle's physics, represented a figure of intellectual oppression. Communism, as an Idea, involves the real of a politics of emancipation. So you start with the situation as it is. That situation is a historical product that doesn't necessarily have to be plunged in any particular darkness. There have been significant events and people who were positively driving forces of emancipation, from Spartacus's revolt to Rosa Luxemburg or Mao's people's war, by way of Toussaint Louverture, Marx, Varlin, Guevara, Lumumba, and tens of thousands of

---

[9] Alain Badiou, *The Meaning of Sarkozy*, trans. David Fernbach (London and New York: Verso, 2008), 100.

others. So we've got a history of emancipation that does indeed exist. And I'm simply saying that the contemporary historical moment of this history of emancipation will be achieved under the name of communism for reasons having to do with its inner essence, that's all.

A. Finkielkraut: But from the glorious revolt of Spartacus to the terrifying people's war of Mao, who thought he could write the remarkable poem of the revolution on a blank sheet of paper, all the situations you mention are binary confrontations. But what do you make of complicated, inextricably tangled human situations? What do you make of quandaries? What do you make of choices that are not between good and evil but between a number of competing goods? What do you make of the tragic? What do you make of differences, nuances, ambiguities, and anything that deviates from the rigid model of the opposition of contraries? In your culture, or should I say your militant imagery, is there a place other than that of betrayal for compromise or, as it's defined by Michel Rocard, the partial attainment of the objectives pursued often at the price of significant concessions to the opponent's objectives? If you accord value only to the events you mentioned, that means that politics for you is still what it was for Robespierre, namely, the great theater where virtue and crime collide. Sometimes that *is* the case, but only at exceptional moments.

A. Badiou: Sure. But those exceptional events punctuate or open up, in what is indeed a condensed and dramatic form, long intermediate sequences in which the norms of political work are clarified and set. That's how I see things. So I'm not saying that war is the only form of politics! I don't think so at all. I simply think that there are events that interrupt the flow of things in such a way that, at a given moment, one particular category or view of things can be said to be the order of the day. What I want to come right out and say is that "communism," in a new form, different from both the historical meaning it had in Marx's work and the statist meaning it had in the twentieth century, is the order of the day. And, naturally, this presupposes a wide variety of tasks, projects, types of organization, and so on. This doesn't mean the war of all against all but rather that the consequences of this fundamental, philosophical form of emancipation need to be brought out and incorporated, through specific political actions, into the world as it is. And, once again, I really can't see why you're so adamantly opposed to this, because, in a way, it means that humanity is a lot more commensurable with the collective or individual truths it's capable of than with the system of organization of its economy. In fact, one of the big failings of all the governments that went by the name of "communist" in the past century was that they combined a despotic state-form with a supposedly collectivist but in fact essentially ineffective form of economy.

A. Finkielkraut: Let's forget about that earlier form for a moment, then, and read what Alain Badiou says: "Without the perspective of communism, without this Idea, there is nothing in the historical and political future of such a kind as to interest the philosopher."[10]

---

[10] Ibid., 115.

The idea, *the* philosopher: these two majestic singulars do not augur well for human plurality. And they simply ignore some very great philosophers who most certainly did not think from the perspective of that idea: I could mention Lévinas and Rosenzweig, for example.

A. Badiou: What are their contributions to political philosophy?

A. Finkielkraut: There are some.

A. Badiou: That's debatable . . .

A. Finkielkraut: I think that any reflection on totalitarianism has much to gain from a reading of Lévinas' *Totality and Infinity*.[11] But, since you're talking about political philosophy, other names, such as Hannah Arendt, Leo Strauss, Claude Lefort, and Cornelius Castoriadis, obviously come to mind. And what I wonder about, when I read or listen to you, is: What place do you allow for someone who doesn't agree with you? The democrat, Camus said, is modest: "He admits to a certain degree of ignorance and recognizes that his efforts possess characteristics that are in part risky and that he does not know everything. And because he admits that, he recognizes that he needs to consult others, to complete what he knows with what they know."[12] In France, that modesty, combined with that praise of conversation, dates back to Montaigne. Indeed, one can read in his *Essays*: "It is to

---

[11] Emmanuel Lévinas, *Totality and Infinity*, trans. Alphonso Lingis (Pittsburgh: Duquesne University Press, 1969).

[12] Albert Camus, "Democracy is an Exercise in Modesty," trans. Adrian van den Hoven, *Sartre Studies International* 7/2 (2001): 12–14.

---

put a very high value on your surmises to roast a man alive for them,"[13] and one can also read: "To my taste, the most fruitful and most natural exercise of our minds is conversation ... When I am contradicted it arouses my attention, not my wrath. I move towards the man who contradicts me: he is instructing me. The cause of truth ought to be common to us both."[14] As far as the proponent of the communist hypothesis is concerned, *the case is closed*, and anyone who disagrees with him must necessarily be in favor of continued inequality – that is, evil. The proponent of the communist hypothesis therefore moves toward the other person not to be instructed but to crush him.

A. Badiou: Once more, I think that's totally wrong. Communism as I conceive it is based on an ontology of multiplicity, not of totality. Consequently, internal and external discussion is a priority topic for me when it comes to the question of antagonism. And, in fact, it's within a space of discussion that polarities likely to become the focus of conflicts may emerge, especially if they're attacked. Something I often comment on is the fact that, when violence is the order of the day, it can only be a defensive kind of violence, a way of protecting what the community has achieved, and in no case a form of attack or aggression. Moreover, and this is a bit of a personal reference, if you look at my *Pocket Pantheon*[15] you'll see that I'm capable of having a sort

---

[13] Michel de Montaigne, *The Complete Essays*, ed. and trans. M. A. Screech (New York: Penguin, 1993), 1167.
[14] Ibid., 1045–7.
[15] Alain Badiou, *Pocket Pantheon: Figures of Postwar Philosophy*, trans. David Macey (London and New York: Verso, 2009).

of fraternal feeling for those who don't share my views at all. That's even my attitude toward *you*, here at the end of our discussion!

AL: *As we come to the end of this "confrontation," the big debate about "national identity," launched at the request of Nicolas Sarkozy in fall 2009, has fizzled out. A huge wave of protest scuttled this initiative that both of you commented on extensively at the beginning of the discussion. What conclusions do you draw from it?*

A. Finkielkraut: In this national identity debate France felt threatened by having to look itself in the face and take notice of what was happening to it. The *doxa* warded off the threat, the media's and academia's desire *not to know* prevailed, and the doctrine of wonderful, salutary multiculturalism won out – at the very time that the foundations of our ability to live together are being rocked by the violence exploding in more and more schools. So in conclusion, and as a belated response to one of your questions, Alan Badiou, I would say that *I'm* not the one who's playing into the hands of the extremists and demagogues; it's the people who, because of their guilty consciences or just through force of habit, calmly chalk up the violence to colonial, post-colonial, or capitalist violence. In that regard, nothing seems more pathetic to me than the attitude of these teachers today who excuse their attackers and pin the blame solely on the government.

A. Badiou: In this case, too, I'm not one of the people you're targeting, because I don't regard the existence of outbreaks of violence in schools, gangs in the housing projects, and so on, as a mere by-product of social phenomena, and I'm far from regarding it as a positive thing. If you take a closer look at it, it's not so much caused by capitalism as it is a mirror image of it. It's the reverse form of it, because, to a very great extent, it's a question of subjective corruption. These young people, whose only ideal is a static, nihilistic one unable to base itself on anything other than commodity circulation, are subjectively devastated. I can't see why I'd make them a paradigm of anything whatsoever. I have, moreover, written a text on the systematic figures of youth, in which I explicitly say that the attempt to reduce all this to social phenomena actually misses the whole point. That's the first thing I wanted to mention. The second is my conviction, which you obviously can't share, that France is finished. I sense that this country, my country, which I love, has come to the end of its cycle of historical existence. I myself feel nostalgic for it, I'm caught up in this negative process. I'm an old French patriot, but I think it's all over, and that's why I'm seeking a solution that could salvage something. I think that solution might be a fusion of France and Germany that would create a type of power comparable to those now developing in the world – China, India, and Brazil – but would at the same time preserve our intellectual, philosophical, scientific, and artistic heritage. However, I feel as if none of the political forces competing for state power – really, not a single one of them – has any plan for what to do about this. None of them has any real idea about what France might become in today's world, in the capitalist game such as it is. And Europe is a shoddy construction, hitched to the wagon of American decadence. My conclusion is that the only thing that can still connect the name "France" with something important is the ability to invent a new internationalism. France has no chance of saving itself as a particular country and as a state. Given the paradoxical capital of intellectuality and political tradition it possesses abroad, however, it may still be able, with a last-ditch effort, to come up with something new where our collective destiny is concerned. France may after all be – in exactly the way Marx called it the classic country of class struggle – the place where a new figure of communism is thought and proposed. That might be its final contribution to generic humanity.

A. Finkielkraut: I, for one, take no joy in noting that we've entered a post-national era. It's probably because France is coming undone that I feel the sort of compassionate patriotism for it that Simone Weil spoke about. What I deplore today is the way the politically correct crowd is bent on attacking this affection. It only exacerbates that melancholy of mine that you picked up on throughout our discussion.

A. Badiou: When I attribute that melancholy to you, it's always with a secret inclination on my part to share it, as I think you've understood. And I would even go so far as to define a whole part of what I do as a vigorous struggle against that melancholy.